The
Kid
Turned Out Fine

The
Kid
Turned Out Fine

Moms Fess Up about Cartoons, Candy,
and What It *Really* Takes to Be a Good Parent

Edited by
Paula Ford-Martin

Adams Media
Avon, Massachusetts

Published by Adams Media, an F+W Publications Company
57 Littlefield Street
Avon, MA 02322
www.adamsmedia.com

ISBN 10: 1-59869-186-4
ISBN 13: 978-1-59869-186-3

Printed in the United States of America.

J I H G F E D C B A

To Cassie and Kate—my very fine girls.

Contents

Contents

Acknowledgments This book was the brainchild of the insightful and talented Kate Epstein, who recognized both the therapeutic value and the comic relief of offering moms the opportunity to share their war stories. I thank her for her vision and patience. My heartfelt appreciation also goes out to the scores of women—from newly minted moms to grand-mothers—who submitted stories for this anthology. Your tales were funny and honest, and each one will hold a special place in my mind and heart. Finally, a big thank-you to my daughters and husband, who put up with many late nights of work on this project and forbade me to feel guilty about it.

Introduction

Every mother should know—the odds are very good that your child will roll off the bed at least once in his infancy. The very day you retire the baby swing, your daughter will fall off the big kid swing set. And the one time you decide it's safe to visit the bathroom while your three-year-old plays quietly in his room, he will lick the household pets and cut his baby sister's hair with blunt scissors.

From day one, childhood is full of bumps, bruises, and questionable "experiments," despite constant maternal surveillance, adherence to parenting texts, and due diligence to both physical and emotional safety.

Of course, in the overwhelming majority of these cases, kids bounce back and move on without a second thought. In fact, in all the tumbles and missteps of childhood, Mom usually ends up bearing more scars and battle fatigue than her child does.

Real mothers have to make real choices in raising our children—choices that sometimes buck popular opinion, sometimes not. In *The Kid Turned Out Fine*, they tell how they cope with the consequences.

This is not an advice book. In fact, in many ways it is an anti-advice book. Reading Drs. Sears or Spock is something most moms do, but taking guidance as gospel from people who have spent little or no time with your children is, well, not advisable. Moms need to decide what is right for them, their kids, and their families. That may mean choosing to do things a little differently than the playbook of the moment, and ignoring those "helpful tips" from friends.

The contributors to this volume, all veterans of the "mommy wars" themselves, offer us a measure of absolution for the guilt that seems to be integral to every mother's DNA. So pop a tape in the VCR for the kids, order out pizza for dinner, and sit back and enjoy. *The Kid Turned Out Fine* is group therapy, stress management, and reality parenting boot camp all rolled into one.

The Tooth Fairy Drops the Ball

By Gina Knudson

My entry into the great parade of mothers had been smoother than expected. I had completed the initiation rites of breastfeeding, given baby her first bath, and could slip a Onesie on a miniature human with less muscle tone than a bowl of mashed potatoes. I had never once driven off with my newborn atop the car. I had this motherhood thing licked. Or so it seemed. Then the child's baby teeth started falling out, and I had to face an ugly fact—I am the worst tooth fairy on Earth.

The curious but time-honored ritual started with complications right from the get-go. Carly literally lost her first tooth when it dropped into a hole I'd been excavating for a shrub. We searched for hours, but the blasted thing had dissolved into the earth. I encouraged the forlorn five-year-old to write a letter of explanation to the kindly tooth fairy. Had the fairy quietly stolen away with the note, leaving some spare change in her wake, the whole mess might have been salvaged.

But the howl in the morning was unmistakable. "The tooth fairy didn't come!" Carly wailed.

"Well, um, honey," I explained, as my husband glared at me accusingly. "I'll bet she needed permission to take a note when there's no tooth under the child's pillow."

"Permithon from who?" she asked.

"The tooth fairy committee, sugar pie. Now never you mind about that. Leave the note tonight, and I know she'll take it."

The mystical fairy did in fact redeem herself, leaving a quarter and a thoughtful note. But she didn't learn her lesson. Two more teeth came out, and were carefully wrapped in tissue paper. Yet sunrise after sunrise, Carly awoke to find the dental relics lingering under her pillow.

"You have to understand," I interceded for the worthless fairy, "we live a long way from any big towns. It probably takes the tooth fairy an extra day to get here—just like the FedEx man."

This was a valid explanation. We live near the Continental Divide in what could be described as a hamlet. But the comparison seemed plainly unsatisfactory to the kindergartner.

Carly has only one baby tooth left, and I have yet to execute a seamless tooth fairy performance. The most recent episode, involving a bicuspid, was as disastrous as the rest.

"The tooth fairy took my tooth, but there's no money!" Carly bellowed one fateful morning, the air whistling through the gaps in her teeth.

"Now angel, why don't you go use the potty and let me have a look. You know you have a hard time finding things," I reminded her gently. As she moseyed to the bathroom, I dove headfirst toward her piggy bank, à la Pete Rose. I robbed as many coins as I could shake from the pink plastic piggy bank, shoved them under her pillow, and nabbed the tissue that had mercifully become tangled (and hidden) in the sheets.

"Look again," I urged smugly. Carly did, and greedily counted the coins she had somehow overlooked moments earlier. "The tooth fairy left me one dollar and . . . thirty-three cents," she announced. "I'm going to tell Dad."

I meekly followed her into the kitchen. "The tooth fairy left Carly a buck thirty-three," my husband said, taking a big swig of the coffee I make (without fail) each morning. "Isn't that a strange amount?"

"Late fees," I offered, wondering how I got saddled with this inane job.

Not even the extra payment made that deal right. Later that night, while the non-tooth-fairy dad tucked Carly in, they found the tooth that had apparently escaped from its tissue-paper wrapper.

"Carly found a tooth in her bed," the unhelpful father said.

I inspected it carefully as our daughter, sensing my expertise in these matters, looked to me for direction. "This looks nothing like Carly's tooth," I pronounced decisively. "The tooth fairy must have dropped another kid's tooth when she visited last night."

This concept was clearly as revolting to the little girl as one of my earlier theories—that the tooth fairy uses children's teeth to build her ivory palace.

"Give me that," I said, snatching the tooth. "I'll give it to the FedEx man."

• • • • •

Gina Knudson is a freelance writer living in the beautiful mountains of Salmon, Idaho. She has two children, including a six-year-old son who still has all his baby teeth. Carly, now eight, is turning out fine despite having a faulty tooth fairy.

I Thought You Were Dead, He Said

By Maureen Mackey

In our quest to be perfect mothers, we struggle to shield our children from the harsh realities of life, of which death is perhaps the harshest. Far from perfect, I blundered more when I tried to protect my sons from having to deal with death than I did when I let them confront it. I learned no matter how hard we wish we could do it for them, children have to come to terms with death and loss in their own ways. And sometimes they can even teach us a few things in the process.

I'm not sure very young children can even understand the concept of death. My younger boy, Adam, certainly didn't. When he was a preschooler I enrolled him in a parks and recreation district class. Once I was late picking him up because of a fender-bender on the road ahead of me. The teacher must have been in a hurry to leave that day. She left me a note on the door and took him to the office, where a child-sized table was set up with crayons and coloring books.

As I ran down the hall, I berated myself mercilessly. How could I expect a four-year-old to understand traffic delays?

• •

I pictured my little boy anxious and afraid, beside himself with worry. When I arrived, no more than ten minutes late, he was coloring a picture. I launched into a torrent of apology.

"Oh hi, Mommy," He looked up from his coloring. "I thought you were dead," he added nonchalantly.

I explained that being late and being dead were vastly different things, but he seemed unconcerned. Soon after, his favorite word became "abandoned." Every deserted house or empty car he saw he proclaimed abandoned—he loved rolling the word around in his mouth. Of course, I took it as a personal reproach, and a direct result of my being late that afternoon.

I'd like to think his casual acceptance at an early age of being on his own in the world has something to do with the independence and nonchalance that persists to this day. But at the time his response to the situation took me aback. Was I such a bad mother that he figured, oh well, she's gone, c'est la vie? It was only later that I realized his fatalism was probably due, at least in part, to what has become known in our household as the "Aquarium Incident."

When Zack, our older son, was five, we decided to get an aquarium. I had read about the calming effect fish swimming in a tank of water could have on children, and I fondly imagined it would be just the thing to settle our rambunctious little boy. Zack watched as we assembled the ten-gallon tank, filled it with colorful rocks and a 3-D backdrop, and added the water and plants. Then it was off to the pet shop, to carefully assemble our little fish community: two angelfish, a couple of gouramis, a small school of neon tetras, and a catfish for clean-up duty.

Sure enough, Zack was fascinated. But it wasn't so much by the fish as the mechanism of the filter and the heater at the back of the tank. Noting his interest, his father showed him the thermometer, and how we regulated the heat to mimic the balmy waters of the fishes' tropical home.

One typically busy morning as I was cleaning I noticed something about the aquarium didn't look right. The fish looked, well, pale. A few tetras were floating on the surface upside down, never a good sign with fish.

I checked the water and it was warm—really warm. The fish were cooking. Then I saw the dial on the heater was up.

I knew it was my curious boy, who loved to turn dials. He didn't know what he was doing. I blamed myself entirely—I should have explained things better to my bright, active son.

I opened the lid and turned the heat down. Surreptitiously I removed the dead fish—I didn't want to upset him with the sight of those little inert bodies. I went to the pet shop and purchased some replacements. Then I walked Zack over to the tank, put my arm around him, and warned him in the gentlest way I could think of about the dangers of messing with the equipment.

"Don't touch the heater knob at the back of the aquarium, honey. If the water gets too hot the fish won't be happy. We wouldn't want that, would we?"

He shook his head, but his eyes were on the knob.

· ·

The next day, I came back, and again a nice little fish boil was going on. Once again his little fingers had found the knob.

An experienced mother would have given up at this point. But I was still a novice. In our family Zack's position as oldest child conferred the solemn duty to shatter any fond, preconceived notions about child-rearing his parents may have and show them the true rigors and rewards of the toughest job in the world.

Again I removed the dead fish before he saw them. "Zack," I called him over, struggling not to raise my voice. "Now, honey, I told you not to touch that knob. If the water gets too warm, the fish won't like it." I purposely made my tone severe. "It could even hurt them."

He looked at me with big eyes. Those eyes were fixed on my hands as I checked the adjustments for the filter and the heater.

I bought more fish. And the next day I found them floating on the surface of the spa-temperature water. Now here's the part where I forever blew my chances of making "mother of the year." I grabbed my five-year-old and marched him to the tank.

"Look," I said, my voice shrill. "See those fish? They're dead, all dead! The water's way too hot. You fiddled with the knob and now you've killed them!"

He didn't burst into tears. He looked at me like I was demented, which I was for a few minutes.

And yet I believe that telling the truth was much better than covering up the evidence. I believe he finally understood what I had been pussyfooting around about. He's certainly grown up to be extraordinarily kind to animals. He'll take a spider outside rather than stomp it, and he's the only one in the family who's ever gotten a squirrel to take food from his hand.

I took the surviving fish back to the pet shop, and dismantled the aquarium. Those knobs and dials were just too tempting for a busy-fingered five-year-old to resist.

Whether I traumatized him that day by confronting him with the dead fish I'll never know. But it traumatized me. Despite the occasional "free" goldfish in a bowl, we never have installed another aquarium. And to this day I can't poach a fish for dinner without remembering and regretting the "Aquarium Incident."

While Zach's fish fatalities didn't seem to faze him, the next death in our family's life hit much closer to home. When both Zach and Adam were still in grade school, their teen-aged cousin contracted a severe form of leukemia. Since my brother and his family live in a small town, my nephew often stayed with us during his two-year battle with the disease while he underwent daily treatments at our local university hospital.

My nephew fought bravely, but he died during a bone marrow transplant in a distant city. I had to explain to my boys what had happened. Adam was nine.

I fumbled with an explanation about the pending funeral, and where people go when they die, trying to be as honest and true as possible. But to Adam it was simple.

"Don't worry, Mommy, he's not really gone," Adam explained to me with absolute certainty. "It's like when you move. The house is empty, but the people in it just went someplace else."

He and his brother mourned their cousin, but I believe they understood better than many of us that death is just a part of the mystery of life. Perhaps their early brushes with death in those earlier, trivial circumstances prepared them in some way.

All I know is that I can't take credit for their insights. I'm just humbled by them.

• • • • •

Born in Los Angeles, **Maureen Mackey** went to University of California Santa Barbara and Berkeley earning degrees in English and journalism. She has authored several historical romances and mystery novels, and writes articles for magazines and newspapers. She lives in Portland, Oregon, with her husband and sons. Visit her at *www.maureenmackey.com*.

Room Service

By Deborah A. Lamontagne

Our daughter Kamrynn, who recently turned seven, is a "hard" sleeper. You could run a freight train through her room and she would merely roll over, pat a yawn, and sigh as she continued wandering through her dream of the moment. We have never had any "sleep" or "bedtime" quandaries and pretty much felt at ease that once tucked into her blankets and headed into her dreams, she would sleep through the night, disturbing no one. Our nightly retreat into her room to check on her before our "bedtime" almost always found her in the same position as when we tucked her in hours earlier.

Several years ago, when Kamrynn was not quite two, we traveled out of town for a family get-together and stayed in a local hotel. We had decided to stay in a suite with an adjoining door to another suite occupied by my sister and her family. After the day's festivities and returning back to the hotel, a few of us decided we wanted to visit a while longer. My husband and I went through our bedtime ritual with Kamrynn and tucked her in tight.

We had always been comforted by the fact that she slept like a rock, which prompted the thought that the late-night visit next door would be "safe." After all, Kamrynn had never awakened during the night before and we were just a few feet from her.

We made sure she was fast asleep. We then headed next door to my sister's room, leaving the adjoining door to both rooms open a wide crack so that we'd be within earshot on the slim chance Kamrynn might awaken.

Around midnight I decided to check in on Kamrynn and see how she was doing on her first night in a hotel bed. Imagine the horror and alarm I felt when I looked in the bed and didn't see her! I couldn't remember leaving on the bathroom light, and when I noticed it on, I thought perhaps she'd ventured in there. When I turned to head toward the bathroom, my heart raced as I saw the door to our room open!

I then realized we had neglected to lock our hotel-room door before going next door, believing that Kamrynn was too small to open it herself. I immediately ran into the hall and when I didn't see her, I began running up and down the halls yelling her name. My other family members all heard me and within seconds my entire family was running the halls of the hotel yelling for Kamrynn. We were in a low-crime area and I didn't seriously fear for her safety, but it was December and the temperatures outside were well below zero. If Kamrynn was able to open the room door, maybe she was able to open an exterior door and head outside!

After what seemed like a million minutes of racing the halls and yelling for her, one of my sisters found me and told me that Kamrynn had been found by another hotel guest and was in the manager's office. Apparently, someone who had just checked in and was in our hallway, found my daughter out in the hallway and had taken her to the manager's office.

I raced to the hotel lobby and when I arrived in the manager's office and saw Kamrynn sitting behind a big desk, swiveling in her chair with a huge smile on her face, as if she'd just been on the adventure of her lifetime, I ran to her, hugged her close and I don't think I let go of her for the remainder of the night.

The hotel staff were moments away from going door to door in the hotel, saying they would have started with guests with the last names beginning with "L" first, as Kamrynn did have her initials K.L. on the label of her PJs.

I have never repeated the mistake of "assuming" my daughter is fast asleep and safe in her bed. It took several months before I could go to bed in our own home without checking in on her many, many times. She's now seven and even now I pass by her room several times a night just to make sure she's still tucked in, safe and sound.

I'm thankful each time I recall this story, for the people involved that kept my child safe and for the angel that was at her side that night. Kamrynn seems not to recall anything about that night. And any late-night visits in hotel rooms are now done in OUR room. After all, we can visit and talk and laugh as we wish, since, as I say, Kamrynn sleeps like a rock and isn't disturbed by any of it . . . right?

• • • • •

Deborah A. Lamontagne is the mother of two daughters, ages twenty-four and seven and has been married for over seven years to husband Ron. She enjoys family gatherings, curling up to read anything by Nicholas Sparks, and watching (and cheering on) daughter Kamrynn's soccer games. She credits her older daughter with keeping her "hip" and her younger daughter with keeping her active.

Baby's Bedtime

By Sandra L. Giordano

edtime is anything but a lullaby at my house. While most parents look forward to putting their babies to bed, I cringe at the idea.

I know theories on "putting baby to bed" run rampant. I have read up on nearly all of them. I am beginning to think the baby experts lost sleep thinking up these sleep-inducing strategies. I would much rather let my baby stay up late until his little body drops from exhaustion. I admit this is probably not good parenting.

I have friends who brag that their children follow such "book perfect" bedtime rituals and then go right to bed at seven P.M. One friend proudly boasts that her little toddler even walks himself up to bed and tucks himself in nightly, soon after she reads him one short story on the family couch. I figure she's either lying or very lucky.

My bedtime scenario goes something like this . . .

"Okay, little Joey it's time for bed."

"Nooooo—Wiggles!" He protests.

"Joey, we've just seen the Wiggles two times already."

"I—want—the—Wig-gles!" It takes a few minutes for my twenty-one-month-old son to produce a whole sentence like this, but he manages to mouth it out and make his point. While I'm proud that he is talking more and more in full sentences, right now I just want him to go to bed. It's been a long day and I still have a long night of paperwork ahead of me.

"No more Wiggles," I say, assuming the "mean mommy" role and taking the videotape that he holds so covetously away from him. "We'll watch more Wiggles tomorrow okay? The Wiggles are going to sleep now. So, Joey has to go to sleep too," I tell him.

"Nooooo!" He cries desperately. "I-want-that."

"Enough Joey." I scoop him up and carry him as he flails his arms and legs, wailing the whole way up the stairs to the bedroom.

"Look, you can wear dinosaur PJs tonight," I tell him.

"Dino!" He says jovially as if the tantrum had never occurred. I always find it fascinating how children turn their emotions on and off like light switches.

"Yes, a big green dinosaur. Let's get ready for bed now," I respond, relieved that the crying has stopped. I undress Joey as he wriggles his way out of his two-piece jogging set, and then lay him down to remove his diaper. Instantly, he kicks himself up like a coiling spring, grabs the pajama shirt from me, and starts jumping on the bed yelling, "Rrrooar" while pretending to be a dinosaur. I giggle, since he does look funny bouncing about naked. The novelty soon wears off for me, but not for Joey, who has enough energy to do this little show all night long.

"Okay, okay, come to Mommy and give me your shirt."

"Noooo!" He squeals out with delight and jolts away, running from one end of the bed to the other.

"Joey, don't make Mommy mad!" I tell him sternly, but calmly. Then I jump onto the bed and grab his little leg. He falls flat on his belly, giggling all the more. I keep him down long enough to put on a clean diaper and pajamas. Out of breath from this energetic effort, I now begin the let's lie down and go to sleep process.

Joey doesn't sleep in a crib anymore. He left it at nine months when he decided it wasn't roomy enough. So, to keep him in bed, I have to lie down next to him until he falls asleep.

I know I've broken another important rule. It goes something like this: "It's important that children learn how to sleep on their own." I also broke the "let them cry it out" rule. I was just too much of a mushy mommy to let an infant cry himself to sleep.

I turn out the lights and prop Joey onto a pillow and rest my weary head. I also hug him tightly so he won't scurry off. All seems fine for about thirty seconds. Then, it dawns on Joey that the lights are out. "Mamma—dark. I—scared," he says using a line he so aptly learned from his big sister.

"Okay, Joey. I'll put the lights on." No sooner do I flip on the night-light, than Joey rediscovers the collection of teddy bears resting on the bureau.

"Look, Mamma," he says with newfound joy. "Bears! Bears!"

"I see them, Joey. Come on. Lie down and let's go night-night."

Pointing to a soft, white bear that is almost the size of him, he repeats "I–want—that!" until I finally give in and get it for him.

"All right. Now, let's put bear to bed with Joey." At this point, I, the bear, and Joey lie down to renew our efforts. Within a few minutes, all is quiet, save for the delicate humming of the TV and the "tippity-tip" of our Poochie's nails as she walks across the wooden floorboards in the hallway.

"Mamma! Mamma!" Joey breaks the near silence with urgency in his little strident voice.

"Sssh, Jo Jo," I say as my sanity begins to unravel itself like a ball of yarn found by a playful kitten.

"Mamma! Mamma!"

"What is it?"

"Poochie up—up."

"Yes, Poochie is up."

"Nooo, Mamma," he repeats frustrated that I don't understand him. "Poochie—up-up" and he pats his hand on the bed.

"Oh, Joey! *Poochie, come on up!*" I yell out in exasperation to our little black terrier. I too start patting the bed in an attempt to get the dog in bed with us. Poochie's paws are heard prancing across the hall and in one instant plop, she lands on the bed and curls up between Joey's feet and my knees.

• •

With growing agitation, I try to rest my head on the pillow.

"Nice—nice—Poochie," Joey keeps saying to the dog as he briskly tugs her tail.

"Joey, Poochie will nip you if you continue to do that. Leave her alone. Let Poochie go night-night." But my words land on deaf ears as Joey just continues tugging the dog's tail and then tries to pull her nails out from under her paws. At this, Poochie lets out a frantic yelp and leaps off the bed, running down the hall in search of a safer sleeping haven. I'm just about ready to join her and leave Joey alone.

"In God's name, Joseph it's time to *go to bed*," I yell, knowing all too well that yelling only adds insult to injury. As the experts point out, it can damage a child's delicate self-esteem at this age. But, I don't think that these so-called experts ever had to put a strong-willed child like my son to bed. Then again, if they followed their own advice, they probably didn't have an anti-sleeping monster like the one I created.

Now I resort to threats. "If you don't go to sleep within the next two minutes, I'm calling your father and then you will have to go to sleep with Daddy." Here I go again, breaking the "never pit child against other parent" theory—a double whammy as I preface my threat with "Stop being a bad boy." I take a deep breath to calm myself and try again.

"Mamma," says Joey patting me on the head like a dog. He now touches and names the parts of my face. "Mamma—aiy-ees. Mamma—chin-chin," he continues. "Mamma—nose," and then, he pinches my nostrils shut. At this, I just about lose it.

• •

"Joseph!" I yell at him. *"What are you doing? Go to bed now!"*

At this, Joey breaks down and begins to cry hysterically calling out "ba-ba."

"Okay, okay, I'll get you a bottle," I tell him, even though I know he's getting too old for it. I feel guilty for screaming so harshly, so I trek down to the kitchen and quickly fill a milk bottle as Joey continues crying loud enough for me to hear him.

"Mamma's coming, Joey. Hold on," I call out to him reas-suringly from the bottom of the stairs. Tired and frustrated, I hand the bottle to my son. He stops crying, begins sucking his bottle, and gently clutches onto a strand of my hair as I lie down next to him.

When my heart stops beating rapidly from the stress, I real-ize that Joey is calming down. I turn to my little boy and whis-per, "Joey, I'm sorry. Mamma still loves you." The Jekyll/Hyde syndrome, as my husband calls it.

He takes the bottle out of his mouth and looks at me with a mischievous, yet whimsical smile. "Mamma," he says back to me.

"Sssh Joey! You go to sleep okay?"

"Mamma," he says.

"What Joey?" I say starting to get annoyed again.

"Mamma—Aiy—wuv—you."

Matter of factly, he puts the bottle back in his mouth and sucks down all his milk. Within five minutes, he's sound asleep.

I quietly come off the bed, tuck the covers up closer to him, and kiss my sweet little sleepyhead good night as I whisper, "I love you too, Joey."

• • • • •

Sandra L. Giordano has an M.A. in creative writing and is an educational writer for parenting publications. Currently, Sandra continues to work at her most rewarding job, which she says is being a "mommy" to her two children.

Mr. Potato Head to the Rescue

By LINDA THOMAS

A trouble-free trip to the store immobilized me for an hour as I contemplated whether G. I. Joe is an action toy for my four-year-old boy, or one toddler step down a path to carnage and warfare.

I only had three things to pick up. Unfortunately, one of the items on my list was close to the toy department. My little Michael knows how to spell the word t-o-y. And he can spot one from an aisle away. "Oh boy," he yelled with anticipation. "Can I get a toy?"

Many times I've heard that question, and most times I've said no. Today I surprised and delighted him with a yes. "But," I cautioned, "only if it's not too expensive."

Michael ran through the colorful, congested aisles searching for a treasure. At every turn he asked me, "Is this too expensive?" The Rock'em Sock'em Robots? Too expensive. Maybe a Buzz Lightyear water toy? Not today. Michael held up a dozen items. They all cost too much.

As he approached the corner of the toy department, his look of anxiety changed to one of awe. He spotted a G. I. Joe action figure and said, "Wow, he's cool." It was $9.49, but the red clearance sticker had it marked down to $6.64. While I was stuck trying to figure out how they came up with such random numbers for prices, Michael was mentally bringing him home already. He is the "Forward Air Control" Air Force G. I. Joe, complete with a dozen gadgets. He is Michael's new friend.

At home as I struggled to get Joe loose from those annoying plastic twist ties, I looked over his field accessories—the backpack, radio, night-vision goggles, dog tags, helmet, canteen . . . and machine gun.

The box describes it as an M4 rifle with scope. Although tiny, when I finally free it from the box I see that it is very realistic. Michael scrambled to his room to introduce G. I. Joe to his plastic pals Buzz and Woody. I was left with a pile of twist ties, and the realization that I just bought my son his first toy gun . . . a teeny tiny, camouflaged M4 rifle. A small seed of self-doubt starts to germinate somewhere in the guilt center of my brain.

The box proclaimed, "Strategic operations forces contribute their expertise to the United States military in the support of freedom throughout the world." That sounded encouraging. "This is a good toy," I tried to convince myself. There are military men and women who put their lives on the line every day for my freedom, and I am grateful for them.

I tossed the box into the recycling bin. What was I worrying about? I recalled that my two older brothers played with a BB gun when they were younger, and they turned out to be the most kind, responsible men you would ever want to know. I even shot the BB gun a few times. I can still remember the sound the tiny pellet made as it hit a battered tin can and swirled off a fence post on our farm.

I asked my husband if he had a G. I. Joe as a kid. He did not, but he told me about how his friends used to play "rock wars." They went to the park and threw clumps of dirt or rocks at each other. I didn't know him as a child, but today he's an outstanding father and great guy. No harm done from the rock wars.

Just when I felt confident with my bargain toy purchase, I scanned the Internet and found dozens of Web sites devoted to making me feel like I am a bad mom. One site clearly states that G. I. Joe and other war toys are "not appropriate forms of children's entertainment." The site claims that Michael's new friend G. I. Joe "promotes aggression as the best way to settle disputes." Oh dear.

Another Web site claims that "playing with war toys increases inappropriate behavior such as hitting, kicking, and hair-pulling." Michael does those things to his older sister after playing with stuffed animals and crayons. Have I just given him a toy that will make the routine brother-sister brawls even worse?

I read on, "By buying children war toys, the message parents send is that it is appropriate to fight and solve problems

• •

violently. If we give impressionable children toys that imply that war is acceptable, then we send them the message that it is all right to act out feelings using weapons." Wait a minute. Michael doesn't even get the message to brush his teeth, after I hand him his toothbrush loaded with blue mint toothpaste.

Enough secondhand research. Time for fieldwork. I had to find out what effect this toy had on Michael. I did my best mom spy routine to sneak up to Michael's room. The door was opened just enough that I could hear him play.

Michael was speaking for G. I. Joe as his new action toy called out, "Help, I'm lost on a mountain. I want my mommy. Help me!" "I'll save you," said Michael in his best cowboy-doll Sheriff Woody voice. "Let me get Mr. Potato Head to help."

I slowly backed away from the door, and smiled. As long as Mr. Potato Head could help, it seemed I had nothing to fear.

• • • • •

Linda Thomas has been a news anchor and reporter for twenty years and a writer all her life. She wrote her first story, "Lindarella," when she was a first grader. The one-page biography told the story of a little girl who worked on her Iowa farm, while all her city friends played.

Duct Tape

By Cheryl A. Martin

A desperate mommy can be a dangerous thing.

I went in one afternoon to rescue Caroline from her crib and her hated nap time. Granted her nap was as much for Mommy as for her, but at two she'd already started to balk.

I held her close and cuddled to make up for the indignities of her enforced incarceration. Then I noticed it. The warm, wet splotch that was spreading across my stomach.

I panicked. I'm not too proud to admit it. What was wrong with my baby? Had she puked? Why was she so wet? Then I noticed her Onesie seemed a little light in the caboose. I looked around her room. There it was. Her diaper had been tossed out of her crib and lay near a pile of stuffed animals and books. The clumps of poop had missed most of her toys. Lucky me.

How had she unsnapped her Onesie? I looked. She hadn't. The little stinker had unfastened her diaper, wiggled it off her cute little butt, and ditched it and the offending poop. Then she'd settled in to pee all over her bed. Wonderful.

• •

Her nap time, which had been my only "me" time, was now a waking nightmare. I knew I'd pay dearly for my thirty minutes with earsplitting screams and another load of pee-soaked laundry—not to mention an Easter-egg hunt for the poop my daughter had flung near and far in her room.

A few days later she started shucking her diaper at night. Some nights we were able to slip a diaper back on her without waking her up, and other nights we weren't so lucky. Those nights we stripped her bed and went down on hands and knees hunting for poop with the aid of a Pooh night-light. We'd rock her for as long as we could keep our eyes open, hoping that if she were asleep when we put her back down, she wouldn't pull the diaper off again.

Then my mother and her husband, Doug, came for a visit. I was tired from all the late nights of poop hunting and sheet changing. Caroline was hyper and wanted to stay up and play. I won—I am bigger after all—and put her to bed. Then I checked on her an hour or so later. She'd already shimmied out of her diaper and chucked it out into her room. I got her into another one and tucked her back in. Before I went to bed I checked on her once more. Diaper off. Bed wet. Mommy desperate. This was war.

I flung her wet sheet and mattress cover down the steps to the laundry room. I put a clean diaper on her and dug for the duct tape I'd seen in the junk drawer a few days before. Duct tape fixed everything, right? Surely, it could work on daughters who refused to keep their bottoms covered at night. I found the roll and cut a piece long enough to go all the way around my daughter's diaper. I figured if I just put pieces over the diaper sides, she'd find a way out. Satisfied that I'd won, I put her to bed.

The next morning, her baby butt was still covered by the diaper. Of course, it was twisted around her belly like a strait-jacket. She'd spent a good deal of time trying to find a way out, but no such luck. Score one for Mom.

Of course the thrill of victory faded when we had to cut the diaper off and the scissors left a tiny scrape on Caroline's skin. Then I felt like the worst mother in the world. After a few days, she stopped fighting the duct tape. She still screamed during her enforced incarceration—I mean nap—but at least I could turn down the baby monitor and have ten minutes to myself without having a daily poop hunt.

I wonder if anyone would look twice if I got the duct tape out when she starts the unending string of "Why? Why? Why? Why?"

• • • • •

With an energetic three-year-old daughter, **Cheryl A. Martin** seldom knows if she's coming or going. By day she's a graphic designer. By night she works on the novel she hopes to publish. She's grateful each evening when her husband, John, pulls into the driveway of their Indiana home. Reinforcements have arrived.

Letting the Cat Out of the Box

By Paula Ford–Martin

ate loves cats. She loves the way they sound, the silky glide of their fur as she strokes them (in both directions, which they don't particularly care for), and their take-it-or-leave-it attitude, which reflects her own stubborn streak. She was Garfield the cat for Halloween, and still wears the costume at least once a week to bond further with the litter of at least twenty stuffed cats and kittens lining her bed and windowsills.

She also has a one-year-old black kitty named "Nellie," whom she will chase for hours. While her dad and I tried to run interference for the poor cat, we got to the point where if her actions didn't seem to be a risk to feline life or limb, we'd look the other way at the minor indignities Nellie was forced to endure, such as wearing outgrown baby clothes or being placed under a laundry basket so Kate could have a captive audience to share her books and play things with.

One day Kate put Nellie inside a large plastic storage box so she could carry her around more readily by the attached handle. She then put the box down and promptly forgot about it when something else caught her eye. Fortunately Mom found it just in time, all steamed up with what little cat breath she had left. One long lecture and a forced Nellie separation later, and Kate seemed to have learned the importance of oxygen to feline survival.

A gentler Kate appears to have emerged since then, and I see her follow Nellie around or cradle her in her arms, talking to her about preschool or her planned agenda for the two of them. Sometimes Nellie converses with the stuffed cat population, and frequently Kate is a kitty herself, meowing after Nellie on hands and knees.

So I guess I shouldn't have been too shocked to walk into the kitchen and find Kate on all fours with her head in the cat-food bowl, sharing Nellie's lunch. Nellie stood nearby with her head cocked to one side, patiently waiting her turn. After another long talk about nutrition and hygiene, Kate has stayed away from the cat food. But she did get a vet's outfit for Christmas complete with stethoscope and plastic examination tools, and I have a feeling Nellie has been sleeping very lightly these days.

• • • • •

Paula Ford-Martin is the mother of two lovely daughters (Kate, age five, and Cassie, age nine). They live in southeastern Connecticut with their dog, a parrot, and the ever-resilient Nellie, who has one or two lives left.

Boardwalk

By Anne K. Spollen

The sea. Late, boring, golden August. Three dimple-faced children and a car packed with shovels and plastic footwear. We were, at last, part of the throng. We drove and drove until the air changed and the wind carried the scent of salt. A low marigold-colored moon glimmered in the sky. "That's an ocean moon," I said to the groggy faces in the rear seat, "it's different from where we live, in the mountains, don't you think?"

"Does this hotel have Nintendo 64?" my oldest child, Christopher, asked.

"No way. I want Game Cube," Philip, my middle guy responded. "It's got better graphics."

"Do you see the clouds, the water around the moon?" I continued, "sort of like a halo."

"I hope they have a restaurant there," Philip said in a dreamy voice, "the kind where you get free drink refills."

"And all the meals come with toys," Christopher nodded. "Squirt toys. They're the best."

"I just wanna see a mermaid," Emma, the youngest, at three, chimed in. "That's all."

Luckily, our room came with a television capable of only the wobbliest reception so I had no trouble unplugging the boys from their hopes of an electronic trance. Our first two days we spent like any other family stepping straight from Americana: we explored the ocean, paying particular respect to crabs and rocks. Emma built walls in the sand, shrieking as waves consumed her labors, the boys rode waves and poked at heliums of jellyfish ghosting the waters. We took rambling walks. We made chittery small talk with families remarkably similar to our own. We collected shells. We smiled at crookedly winding dune fences, at whimsical fish, at carousels forged to resemble octopi. By the end of the second day, the ceaseless charm and wholesomeness of our seaside villa had begun to grate. I could not shake the disquieting sense that we had landed inside the Disney version of summer.

"What do you think," I asked my boys, "of this place?"

We were eating frozen yogurt at one of the many umbrella tables in front of one of the many stores. I looked down the row of umbrella tables only to see our family multiplied dozens of times.

"It's sort of . . . " Philip said, "like one of those movies you get out of the library for us. You know, all peaceful. Like nothing bad will ever happen here."

"But it's less boring than school," Christopher offered. "So do you like it, Mom?"

"I was wondering," I began, but stopped. "Never mind." How could I explain to these kids that the perpetual perkiness of this oceanside retreat left me feeling common and homogenized as plankton?

Philip, my one child who was a surprise and now delights in surprise, looked up, knowing (and hoping) I was up to something. "Why, Mom?"

"Oh, just that there's another place a bit north of here that I went to when I was younger. It's probably not, well, the best place for a family vacation." I remembered the dash and vigor of the boardwalk, the taut edginess of the people I saw on the boardwalk. As I remembered the sights and sounds of my pre-Mom vacation, I looked up to see a regalia of strollers sailing past. That place up north may have had more pizzazz, but it was also known for its casino nightlife. I imagined the boys trundling back to school using words like "roulette" and "harlequin."

"Probably not the best choice, where I'm thinking," I said finally.

"Do they have go-carts there, at this place?" Christopher asked.

I nodded.

"What about arcades?" Philip asked. "Do they have any arcades?"

I nodded again.

Parenting often leaves me with a sense that I am guessing, that I am constantly hoping my choice is the best one for my kids. But this time, as I sat listening to the deliriously repetitive jangle of carousel music, I looked hard into their faces and I knew what to do. Precisely.

By the time darkness fell, with half our unused room money refunded, we were on our way to the place I remembered, to the place I wanted to show my kids: Atlantic City. It was easy enough to find. The glitter of lights through the dark night lures humans in the exact manner fish are lured through the dark sea by the shimmer of hooks. Only instead of the sudden plunging spangle of a hook, Atlantic City has a sudden rise of light, a place that clearly means to capture the soul.

"Look," Christopher said, staring at an enormous, illuminated statue of Neptune "it's like the sea has come alive."

"You're right," I answered. "It's not the same here, though, as the last place. You're going to have to be a bit more careful. It's more of a . . . city."

"That's okay." He moved his gaze from one larger-than-life building to the next. He nudged his brother who woke and looked around for a few moments. "What do you think?"

Philip blinked for a few moments as he looked around at the dazzle. "It's like we're surrounded by electricity," he murmured sleepily, "completely."

Surrounded by electricity. Not a bad way to end the day.

The casino crowd is a late-night one, so the next morning we were up and out on the beach before most of the hotel guests had woken. My fear that I had taken the kids on a vacation that would get me convicted in a court of more conventional mothers began to abate.

We collected shells, again, and we went for our customary amble down the boardwalk. Only this time, in the silent morning with the gauzy ocean to one side of us and the hardscrabble of litter and pigeons to the other, the boardwalk seemed to act as a margin between dream and waking.

After a few minutes, Philip spotted a man dressed in padded clothing in the August heat. The man stood and peered into the sun, muttering wildly to himself.

"Is he . . . drunk?" Philip asked, obviously struggling to find the right word.

"No," I replied, "but he will be tonight." The boys watched as the man folded up the cardboard that served as his home. Both my boys stood still until the man vanished. I could see the comprehension dawn in their eyes: beneath the glassy largess of the casinos, homeless people sleep on cardboard.

But then the city woke. We fell into step with its rhythms right away. That first day, we established our routine. We bought boogie boards and rode waves alongside other families. We swam in the hotel pool. We bought Emma some shovels and built sand creatures: strange ones, octopi and gobble fish, sea fairies made of bits of shell with seaweed hair. We swam in and out of stores along the boardwalk, watching shop owners, some brittle with suspicion, watch us.

Emma longed to see pirates. I spotted a few men, flashy razzle-dazzle types sporting large rings and brilliantly colored suits, men who had to be gamblers. Their clothing served as a kind of uniform, not terribly different from the parrot-on-the-shoulder, eye patch of seafaring pirates. I considered how these men, like pirates, engendered risk for gold, for the lure of treasure, how they walked the planks of the boardwalk. "Yes," I said, "they're everywhere. Only on land, they wear those suits as a disguise." Emma looked, as a man in a pale peach suit passed by us.

Her eyes got very wide.

One sunless afternoon, we watched clouds drape our twenty-first-story hotel room, and then we walked a few miles from our hotel, out into the city itself. We did not find the quaint bungalows with miniature lighthouse collections on lawns that had comprised the neighborhood of our first, sleepier destination. Here, we walked past row housing and pawn shops, past taquerias and stores whose purpose we could not identify. We stood in front of one such store, trying to guess what it might sell. Sepia light pooled in the shop window. A few dolls sat next to a typewriter, some books leaned in a precarious stack, and several black straw hats lay scattered about. Those were the entire contents of the display.

"A kind of attic store," we decided at last. (We still talk about that store, to this day.)

We walked out behind the casinos, able to see pigeons and gulls pecking around Dumpsters. We noticed that shade on the streets was created from the long rhombus of light shed by the casinos instead of from trees. And then, above this all, we heard a sudden peal of church bells. It was the kind of setting I wanted my children to see: a place of authentic human endeavor, a place that exposed both the beauty and the frailty of our goals. (It could be said that family life exposes the same two qualities.)

We roamed the beaches for the remainder of our days, and when night fell, the air was so charged, it seemed to snap. Philip was right; we were not only surrounded by electricity, we had entered it. We went out in the evenings, eating ice cream on the boardwalk, only instead of seeing mirror images of ourselves, we saw people quite different from ourselves. Feathered and jeweled showgirls waved as they wheeled by on carts. Tourists from all over the world passed us and we exchanged smiles, people dressed in glittery night finery rode past in jitneys without glancing at anyone, women wearing layers of scarves came up to us, offering to read our palms.

Then, during the last night of our vacation, Emma looked up at the garishly arresting facade of the Taj Mahal. She insisted that we had, at last, arrived in the land of Aladdin. No one argued that we had not. That final night we spent at the Steel Pier, going on rides with the ocean beneath and around us. Every time a ride rose into the air, one of the Taj's onion domes came into view. Emma's enchantment was visceral.

"So," I said as we placed the last of our plastic footwear and shovels into the car, "where do you guys want to go next year?"

"Definitely here," the boys said.

"Not to the first place? Didn't you think that beach was more our speed?"

"No. Too much like school," Philip said, "you know, everything safe."

"I want to come here on my birthday," Christopher announced.

"On Christmas Eve?" I laughed. "What would we do with ourselves?"

"Watch clouds bang into the windows," he answered with a slight edge, as though anyone would have guessed this.

We drove away from Atlantic City, pausing at the traffic light next to the statue of Neptune. I had not noticed that first night how darkly serious Neptune's expression had been cast. None of his features had been softened; the tines of his trident not blunted. He was meant to show command and power. We stared into his face for a few minutes, and as we pulled away, I could not help but think how his eyes seemed arrested in contemplative watch, perhaps the most befitting expression for the guard of a city that struggled so patently between seduction and redemption. I knew that the kids would not understand all that they had seen, or most of what I was thinking, but I did know that they had been touched by a place that was authentically human in its diversity, challenge and beauty.

And that's not a bad way to end the summer.

• • • • •

Anne K. Spollen holds an M.A. in literature and has published extensively. Her essays have appeared in several anthologies and both her poetry and fiction have been nominated for Push-cart prizes. She lives in New York with her husband, three children, three cats, and a dog.

Power Nap

By Allison Pattillo

What can I say? I love naps. I like to take naps, I like watching my children take naps, and I love to nap with my children. Well this was all great, until my children outgrew their afternoon siestas. I didn't know what to do! The hardest part of my day was no longer the traditional 5:00 P.M. "witching hour"— it was from 2:30 to 3:30.

I would struggle to stay awake through the afternoon. I ate . . . a lot. I drank tea. I played games with my children. I took the girls on walks. But as soon as we sat down to read a book together, I was snoring away. It probably took me a week to get beyond page five of *Where the Wild Things Are*. It seemed like I would never make the adjustment.

Now my children are seven and five and every now and then, I still have to give in, and I have discovered that my children are okay with that. They know that when Mommy lies down on the sofa, it is time for quiet play. I have awakened on the floor with train tracks built around me and blocks stacked on top of me.

● ●

Needless to say, my stolen naps aren't the best-quality sleep. They are usually more of a rest; I believe my grandmother used to call it "resting her eyes." I am alert enough to fasten outfits onto dolls and mediate arguments, but my daughters know they have to be somewhat self-reliant for a few minutes, while Mommy recharges. We have ground rules while I rest: no scissors, no answering the door, no going outside, no swinging from the chandelier, no playing with matches, etc.

The surprising thing is the fact that my guilty pleasure has turned into a good thing for all of us. Not only do I—the lone night owl in a house of early birds—get a little extra sleep, but my children are discovering how to work and play together. Since this has been so successful, I have discovered a new guilty pleasure—pretending I'm asleep, and listening to my daughters play when they think they're alone. No, it isn't as restful, but listening to their teamwork and knowing of their closeness is much more rewarding.

● ● ● ● ●

Allison Pattillo has been a full-time wife and mom. However, now that her daughters are in school, she is spending more time writing, and deciding what she wants to be when she grows up. She is an avid skier, swimmer, runner, and biker, and lives in Colorado with her family.

How I Won

By Pam Koons

I am so tired of trying to force my kids to wake up and get to school on time. I've tried incentives, alarm clocks, sleeping in their clothes to save time, eating in the car—all the usual mom things that we do, but will only admit to our best friends. That morning struggle got to be so bad at our house, that I decided to put a complete stop to it before I lost my own sanity (or maybe it was insanity that drove me)!

One morning with *no* warning at all, I decided to play hard-ball with my kids and get them to school on time. My strategy was born out of desperation. At least that's how I justified it. We all woke up at the same time, and went through the same rituals of "I don't want to go to school," "I'm not hungry," "I don't feel good," etc. I calmly took a shower, dressed myself, did my makeup, and even put on some jewelry; meanwhile the kids were in stages varying from just getting out of bed to watching TV to still sleeping. Most likely they were waiting for me to yell at them to get moving. I put out their bowls of cereal and fruit without saying one word while they watched me. I ate

• •

my own cereal, and I think they were as close to having a heart attack as grade-school kids can be, as I was not complaining, ordering, or yelling. They knew something was up as I was too cheerful. I'm sure they thought I was letting them out of school for the day! The older ones were puzzled as they looked at the clock and the younger ones were oblivious to what was going on. All they knew was that it was very quiet and that that was "weird."

Then *bam*! The alarm went off and the fun began. I had bought a new alarm that they hadn't heard before and set it to when we always left for school. I calmly said, "It's time to go to school."

And the objections began. The kids complained: "I didn't get my breakfast," and "I'm still in my pajamas," and "I'm not ready." I calmly said, "I *know*," and I took each and every one of them out to the car *in* their pajamas and proceeded to drive them to school. Even though they weren't ready for school, school was ready for them.

Then it got *real* loud. "You aren't really taking us to school in our pajamas!" "What will the other kids think?" then, less loudly, "Please take me home," "I'll get dressed on time tomorrow."

Little did they know I had packed them each a bag of real clothes to change into at school. When we did get to school they were still in their pajamas and had to get out of the van— and I simply handed each one their bag of clothes to change into. But walking into the school in their PJs was just enough to make them remember that this could happen again if they weren't ready in time from now on. I calmly told them to have a nice day. They said little and I could tell they were furious.

All day I felt horrible. Maybe I did the wrong thing, but I knew I had to do something. I waited and waited. I cursed myself. I validated myself. I called my mom (bad idea). Finally they came home, went into their rooms all by themselves, calmly occupied themselves until dinner, and we had a nice conversation about their school day and the like.

When we all woke up the next morning I noticed a significant change right away. They were getting ready for school without me yelling. They got dressed on their own, and they ate on their own. We actually had a bit of pleasant conversation. The alarm went off and everyone was ready to go to school.

I couldn't believe it. I had *won*! Apparently being seen in pajamas at school was worse than having to get up early to get ready. I even had another mother call me to ask me where I got the guts to do it! Word spreads in a small town. I won't say they are now perfect little creatures—but the mornings have significantly improved. All thanks to a little creativity.

● ● ● ● ●

Pam Koons lives in a beautiful Pacific Northwest forest on five acres. Recently, she chose to take early retirement due to health reasons after owning a private school for twenty-two years. Constantly researching new healing approaches has led Pam back to her original passion—writing. She spends time loving her dogs, writing a book on parenting, and keeping calm.

Bare Necessities

BY JOANNIE HINMAN

I was a nervous first-time mom-to-be but felt like I had everything ready for the big day. In planning ahead I washed all of the baby clothes in warm water, using baby-approved detergent and the extra rinse cycle. Unfortunately, there was one step that did not make an appearance on my mental checklist.

While we were in the hospital with my little Zoe, the nurses dressed her in a teeny, tiny diaper, a white cotton short-sleeved Onesie, and a cute little pink hat that had been knitted by some kind hospital volunteer.

My husband and I took our bundle of joy home. We carefully changed her Onesie, her little hat, and her itsy-bitsy diaper. We warmed the wipes to make sure she didn't get a chill on the changing table. We had the black and white mobile so she'd be nice and stimulated in her crib for the one second she spent alone before making a baby noise which came through the monitor we were staring at and sent us dashing for her room. We kept meticulous charts noting when Zoe ate, when she slept, and what was in her diaper. I charted what I consumed, and whether or not Zoe reacted to my milk differently based on what I ate. I wanted to do a perfect job with her.

But something was missing. My mom arrived after we'd been home for about a week. Leave it to Grandma to notice that I had failed to ever put clothing on my daughter. No cute outfits, no footsie jammies, none of the items I had carefully washed and put away in designated drawers with newborn sizes stacked on top of 0–3, which were stacked on top of 3–6.

How can a mom forget *clothing*? It never crossed my mind.

The videos of the first few days of Zoe's life in February in New England show a little six-pound peanut wearing just a T-shirt as her parents pick her up wearing thick cotton sweaters and flannel shirts. Whenever Zoe cries on tape I can hear my voice announcing, "She must be hungry again."

No, Mom. Some of those times she was probably just cold.

Thanks to Grandma, Zoe's been dressed since she was ten days old. Zoe often has an extra sweater or a coat wrapped tightly around her. I think I can trace the history of that inclination, and I have to own it!

Fortunately it's been my only mistake.

• • • • •

Joannie Hinman lives in Rhode Island with her husband, Chuck, and their two daughters, Zoe and younger sister, Lily (who's been well-dressed since birth). Joannie hosts a morning radio show on Coast 93.3 in Providence. Tune in and she'll be happy to tell you the appropriate clothing for the day.

One Mom's Dirty Little Secret

BY GWEN MORAN

My mother has always been one of those women whose home can be photographed for *House Beautiful* at a moment's notice. Her bathrooms glisten, the carpet is pristine, and the kitchen floor is clean enough to eat from. Of course, with four young children, then three grandchildren underfoot for much of her life, there usually is someone eating from the floor, so the latter was probably out of necessity.

I've always been very different from my mother, but I don't think I realized how far apart we'd swum in the gene pool until the day that a friend stopped by my home unexpectedly. Rather than open the door, shining bright sunlight onto the pile of unfolded (but clean) laundry on my couch, the socks (not clean) strewn across the floor, and the thick layer of dust that had somehow settled on just about everything in sight, I hid. Yes, I hid. In my own home. From my friend. So she wouldn't see that my living room looked like a disaster area.

It's not that I'm a particularly messy person. But with a more-than-full-time career, a husband, a three-year-old daughter, and an active social and volunteer schedule, housework falls somewhere between "rotate tires" and "clean gutters" on my mile-long to-do list. Still, it would be nice to have visitors over without needing several months' notice to stow our stuff. Plus, hiding from visitors in one's own home isn't healthy. Realizing that I was at risk of becoming a recluse, I did something that my mother would never have done: I called for help.

I dusted off the Yellow Pages, and opened them up. There, I found a long list of people and organizations ready to help me transform my home into a showplace. I chose the service located farthest away, reducing the chance that someone I knew would show up and discover the state of my upstairs bathroom.

A few days later, right on schedule, a little yellow car pulled up and parked in front of my house. Four women in green polo shirts and khaki pants stepped out of the vehicle in an oddly synchronized manner, retrieved a variety of tools, bottles and buckets from the trunk of the car, and then walked resolutely, single-file, up the walkway. I opened the door.

"Hi, Happy Housekeepers here. I'm Mary, the team leader," said the woman who was clearly in charge. Suddenly, I panicked. How could I let strangers see my home in such disarray?

"Mary, I'm . . . well, I think I've made a . . . ." Mary cut me off. "Honey, just leave it to me. Believe me. However bad it is, we've seen worse." She leaned closer to me and whispered, "I used to clean up crime scenes."

I didn't know whether that was a relief or not, but Mary pushed past me as she assigned one woman to tackle the upstairs bedrooms, one the kitchen, and one to handle bathrooms. Then, she strapped a vacuum canister onto her back and, like some domestic Robocop with a hairnet, began clearing a swath through the Cheerio crumbs my daughter had dropped on the carpet.

I walked from room to room, helpless, yet amazed at the unabashed efficiency of these professionals at work. A few swipes of a cloth and the toothpaste residue disappeared from the bathroom sink faucet. Another couple of swipes and the stairway balusters shined like new. Two hours later, my home was ready for its close-up.

When Mary handed me the bill, it seemed a very small price to pay. I included a generous tip, and loaded the women up on bottled water and Diet Coke, thanking them profusely. I thought of preparing a gift basket, but then figured that would be overkill.

I picked my daughter up from camp and brought her to our tidy domicile. At first, she panicked, concerned that someone had stolen all of her toys. She thought that we had been robbed because the house was clean. I reassured her by showing her the purpose of the closet and toy box—now filled with dolls, stuffed animals, and games.

Two days later, when my family came for dinner, there was no frantic shoving of clutter into closets or last-minute bathroom scrubbing as the doorbell rang. I was calm, cool, and collected when the first guest—my mother—arrived. I could see her blink with surprise. Or maybe it was from the light reflecting off the gleaming hardwood floors.

"Everything looks great, honey," she commented, obviously relieved that I had, indeed, inherited her genetic tendency for tidiness.

For a moment, I thought about fessing up, but then reconsidered. As most successful professionals know, sometimes it's better to outsource, especially when you have access to a provider who can handle the job better than you can. Clearly, these women were more adept with vacuum canisters and antibacterial kitchen cleaner than I would ever be, especially with my family and professional obligations. Instead of feeling guilty about not being able to do everything by myself, I decided that I should feel proud about making a wise household management decision.

Now, my newfound friends visit me just about every other week to give my house a sudsy spruce-up. Because I've learned to open the door wide when they arrive, I no longer feel the need to dead-bolt it shut when a friend stops by out of the blue. And with the time this has freed up, I may even get those gutters cleaned.

I wonder if I can hire someone for that?

• • • • •

Gwen Moran is a professional writer whose work has appeared in *Entrepreneur, USA Weekend, Woman's Day,* and *Family Circle*—but not *House Beautiful* (yet). She is the coauthor of two books, and frequently recounts funny stories about her family at *www.gwenmoran.com.*

In the Pink

By Shelly Nash

Someone once said clothing makes the man. If that's true then I'd say it's obvious that it also makes the woman and the child. Clothing is a way we express ourselves to the outside world. The whole multibillion dollar fashion industry is based on the need and desire people have to make a statement and create their own look. This being said I decided long ago to allow my daughter, even at age five, to pick out her own clothes. No, I don't take her shopping and randomly let her grab anything off the rack that appeals to her, but I do take her with me when I pick out her clothes. I ask her opinion about each item. The conversation often goes like this:

ME: Hayley, what do you think of this cute shirt? It has a pony on it and it's blue. You love blue.

HER: It's ugly. Ponies are for boys or babies and it's more purple than blue. I like this one (picking up a pink shirt—which looks like four other pink shirts she already has).

ME: Ponies aren't just for boys. And you already have a few pink shirts. How about this other red one (holding up a short-sleeved red shirt).

HER: I can't wear a red shirt, Mom. Kelly said people who have red hair like me shouldn't wear red. It makes you look—what do you call it—inviable.

ME: Honey, I think you mean "invisible" and that's not true. Kelly is only seven so she might not be the best person to give you fashion advice.

Kelly is the little girl across the street. Having finished first grade she is much more knowledgeable and worldly than my daughter. Hayley often goes to her for advice on important issues like which new Barbie to ask Santa to bring (she wanted Malibu Beach Barbie but Kelly suggested Doctor Barbie which came with a plastic stethoscope), which Power Ranger is the coolest (yellow or red ranger), and fashion consultations.

"Can't I please just get this pink shirt? It's so pretty! I'll look like a Princess in it!" she twirls around happily holding the shirt.

Needless to say we left the store with three pink shirts, a pink skirt and a peach (too light to really be called pink) pair of Capri pants. Hayley was dressed in her pink Princess outfit when we were getting ready to go and see her grandmother (my mother-in-law) the following Sunday. She cheerfully skipped down the stairs pink as a petunia with three pink ribbons in her hair and her red ruby slippers (the ones purchased to go with her Dorothy costume for Halloween), smiling and humming the theme from *Sesame Street*.

I thought she looked adorable and was about to compliment her on the entire ensemble, when I realized someone in the house disagreed. "Hayley, what are you wearing? You must have dressed yourself again," he says, turning to me with his "I'm annoyed" face and tone. "Why don't you take her upstairs and have her put on something more appropriate?"

"But, Daddy, don't you like my outfit? I look like a Princess! A pink beautiful Princess!" Hayley twirls round and round while waving her hands to heighten the dramatic effect.

"Uh, yes. You look very nice honey but we're going to Grandma's house and I thought maybe you'd put on something--- oh, uh, I don't know, a little less bright. Not so pink."

"But I love pink! It's my favorite color! I wish everything was pink. Mommy said I could wear this."

All eyes turn to me, of course, as if I am the Russian Olympic judge ready to make or break her chances of receiving a gold medal in the fashion competition. Trying to avoid any conflict I just shrug and try to stay out of it. This frustrates my husband. But coming from a man whose closet contains twelve button-down blue shirts, eight pairs of khaki pants, three charcoal suits, and two polo shirts and pairs of jeans (for when he's feeling "crazy"), he really isn't qualified to be her style guru.

"Why don't you go back upstairs and put on that brown dress Grandma gave you on your birthday? I know she'd love to see you wearing it," he tries.

"Brown is ugly; it makes me look stale."

"I think you mean 'pale' sweetheart," I offer.

"Yeah. Pale. I don't want to wear that dress. It's itchy too."

"Then how about that nice yellow jumper thing we bought for you in Florida? You look very nice in that," he says.

"Daddy! That's too small for me now! I'm growing so big. That's why Mommy and I went shopping and got me all these cute new pink clothes. Don't you think I look pretty?"

Hayley did indeed wear her pink Princess outfit that day. My mother-in-law did comment on how "bright" she looked and asked if I thought it was wise to let a five-year-old dress herself (to which I responded "yes" and added that I felt it fostered a sense of accomplishment and stimulated creativity and individuality. She looked at me blankly when I said this and then asked if I'd like to try some artichoke dip and offered me the recipe).

It's not like there's never been a time when my daughter has tried to flex her fashion muscles and I haven't given in. There was the time she wanted to wear her nightgown under her dress to church on Christmas Eve so she could get to bed quickly when we got home and that way Santa wouldn't "skip our house" like he had Kelly's (who is Jewish). Then there was the time she wanted to wear her bathing suit to ice skating because she gets "so hot" skating fast and she knew it would cool her off. We had quite the discussion when she insisted it was okay to wear her soccer uniform outside in January since she saw "those guys on TV wearing soccer uniforms and playing outside."

Barring those few exceptions I do let her choose her own clothes. I am amazed and surprised at the combinations she puts together. Rarely have people made negative comments about her color coordination or texture choices. Usually it's just the opposite. I'll hear the check-out girl at the grocery store say: "I really like that baseball cap you have on. It matches that party dress nicely."

Or the mailman will comment: "Your ballerina outfit looks so pretty with those cowboy boots and hat."

She will smile and say thank you with a sense of pride and accomplishment. And I marvel at what a creative, happy, and secure little girl she's become.

• • • • •

Shelly Nash lives in Glencoe, Illinois, with her two daughters/ stylists/fashion advisors Jessica and Hayley, and her husband, Doug, who thinks periwinkle and magenta are tropical fruits and insists that it's okay to wear socks with sandals.

Brilliant Big Sister

By Shareen Wornson

Our daughters were born fifteen months apart. Our first, Samantha, was an excellent sleeper. She started sleeping through the night when she was three months old. I would nurse her around 10:00 P.M. in our bed and then carry her to her room and put her in her crib. She would sleep there until around 5:00 A.M. the next morning. I would nurse her again and then let her sleep with me until I was ready to get up around 7:00 A.M. It was perfect for me.

Then I got pregnant again, and that took its toll on my sleep schedule. By the time Emily was born, I was pretty wiped out from the back-to-back pregnancies and the rigors of attending Samantha. I was too tired most nights to even get up and reach for her in the cradle next to our bed. And many times I would wake up for her next nightly feeding and find that I was still upright in bed, holding her from the last nightly feeding. So began the habit of letting our new daughter sleep with us.

At first it was just easier. Neither one of us would have to get up in the middle of the night to get her when she wanted to nurse. I barely even had to wake up to do it. She was right there and I would lay her next to me and let her latch on.

I did enjoy the time she spent with us in our bed. Samantha had taught me how fast babies grow. I really wanted to savor every moment for as long as I could. I didn't care if Emily ever walked or talked—I just wanted her to stay my baby forever.

But it became more difficult to have her in the bed, because she was growing and becoming more active in her sleep. I was worried about rolling over on her and suffocating her or hurting her. So, even when she was sleeping longer hours in the night, I was still continually awakened by her tossing and turning. Emily had her own crib, but it was in the room she shared with Samantha. I was afraid to disturb Samantha's good sleep schedule. So, I kept Emily with us, trading my own good sleep for Samantha's.

By the time Emily was fifteen months old I decided it was time to get her out of our bed. I had awoken one night with a foot in the chest and the wind knocked out of me from her evening acrobatics. I decided we would bring Emily's crib into our room and she would sleep there.

Emily decided otherwise. She stood and cried and shook the crib until I couldn't bear it anymore. So I let her back in our bed.

The next night I tried taking the side off the crib. This way she would have access to our bed. Maybe she would feel closer to us without the bars. Not Emily! She wouldn't stay on her mattress. She wanted to be in our bed—period.

The third night I decided all bets were off. Emily was going to sleep in her own crib in her shared room with her sister. We were assured by her pediatrician that her crying would be okay—as long as she was safe and secure. So, we put them both to bed and closed the door.

Emily cried and screamed for two agonizing hours. I made several trips in to assure her it was okay and encourage her to go to sleep, but nothing would calm her. Remarkably, Samantha had fallen asleep to her sister's screaming and seemed completely unaffected by it. But I certainly couldn't. And eventually, I was crying too. I finally went in to get her.

I took Emily *back* to our bed. Emotionally drained, we both fell asleep immediately.

The next night we tried it again. We put the girls to bed and left them. Once again, Emily began her crying and screaming. We let it go and after about twenty minutes she stopped. I was panicked. Did she give herself a heart attack? Had she stopped breathing? I listened at the door. I didn't want to go in if she was actually sleeping and risk waking her up again. I heard Samantha talking. She was saying, "It's okay, Emily. Don't cry."

Very carefully I cracked open the door to see what they were doing. Samantha had climbed into Emily's crib and was patting her back and lying down next to her. It was brilliant! And, it was my two-and-a-half-year-old who made it happen! They slept together like that for the rest of the week. Every night we put them to bed in their own beds and every morning we would find them together in Emily's crib. It was beautiful.

For several years the girls shared a room and spent about half of their time sleeping in the same bed. When they were six and eight we moved into a house and they each had their own room. Even though they fight as siblings will, and even though they have their own rooms, they still spend about half of their nights sleeping together.

• • • • •

Shareen Wornson is a video editor and mother of two daughters. She lives in Dallas, Texas.

Why You Had Children

By Juli Hiatt Caldwell

When you have no children and you decide to go out to lunch, you decide that soup and salad sounds appealing. You wait for your table at the new Italian restaurant, and then leisurely look at the menu while your server takes your drink order. While you wait for your food, you pour over some briefs for your afternoon meeting, or if it's a slow day at work, you flip through that latest fashion magazine, contemplating your autumn color palette or which handbag will look best with the new outfit you just purchased. When your soup and salad arrive, you consume your meal slowly and savor every last bite. You finish, pay your bill, and head back to work feeling refreshed and ready to tackle the rest of your day.

When you have kids, you replace the genial server and charming Italian bistro with anywhere that has a play land. During your ten-minute wait to get to the register, you struggle to keep your kids with you in the serpentine line. They eventually break free, excitedly discussing which toy they might get in their kids' meals as they bounce up and down in front of the toy display. You notice the children in line in front of you are dressed like a rapper you saw spewing obscenities as you flipped through TV channels last night, frantically trying to find the show your child earned (okay, it was actually bribery on your part) by completing his chores without being yelled at 1,200 times. You attempt not to roll your eyes at the little white boy's oversized FUBU jersey as it dangles precipitously above his knees, because you're trying to teach your children not to be judgmental.

When your children's food arrives, your two-year-old notices that her hamburger has come with a pickle. She doesn't *like* pickles. As she wails at the top of her lungs because the pickle has made contact with her food, you rip napkins from their holder and wipe the burger, trying earnestly to convince her that it's all clean and she'll never know it was there once she tastes it. Your older daughter has found the toy that came with the meal, which you generally try to hide until after the food has been eaten, since you know once she gets the toy she won't focus on her meal. The doll she is now playing with is dressed like the TV rapper's girlfriend, and you absentmindedly utter what you're really thinking under your breath. Now you have to explain to your curious four-year-old what a hoochie mama is and launch into an impromptu discussion on modesty and good taste while you reassemble the two-year-old's burger.

You finally get settled down to your lunch—Diet Coke and snatches of what your kids don't eat. The older kids are off playing and as you reach for a lukewarm fry, you look up in horror as you realize that your four-year-old is reciting, word for word, the lecture you just gave her on modesty to another child in the playground, using that imperious tone that only a four-year-old can conjure up, finishing like a pint-sized Napoleon berating his troops and calling the other child's mother a hoochie mama.

The two-year-old begins finger-painting with the ketchup she snatched while you made embarrassed apologies to the other family. You are just humiliated enough that you call all the kids and get ready to leave, hoping your son can hear you in the din and confusion of lunch hour in the play land. You pick up the youngest, and she hugs you fondly and leaves a ketchupy red handprint on your left breast.

Taking a deep breath and counting backward from ten, you wipe it off the best you can and gather your things, trying very hard to avoid the dirty looks the other mother is shooting at you and hoping she doesn't notice the slimy orange-red smear smack-dab on your goods. She looks great, you think, as you glance down at your stretch-marked, ketchup-covered body. She is wearing short shorts and a cropped tank top, proudly displaying her perfect abs and bellybutton ring. Maybe you'll get a bellybutton ring when you get your body back? Uhhhh . . . maybe not.

After loading the kids back into the car, you decide to make one last stop at the bank before you go home. The kids decide to play jump rope with the velvet ropes, and the unsuspecting two-year-old gets whacked in the head with a flyaway rope before you realize what they are doing. Fortunately there aren't too many people in line this time, so using threats that would make grown men shudder, you manage to make them behave long enough to get back to the car. They scream and fight on the way home. You practice your deep relaxation breathing to keep yourself from screaming along with them.

By the time you walk in the door, you have one thought in your mind: you are ready to list the children on eBay, offering free shipping to anyone who clicks the "buy it now" option. As you wipe the stray streak of ketchup from your two-year-old's face and get her settled into her crib her arms encircle you, sleepily. You settle into the couch with some books to read to the older ones, their small arms draped around your shoulder as you open the pages; a little boy whispers in your ear, "I love you higher than the sky," just like you used to when he was a baby, and like your dad did to you. Maybe you won't list them on eBay. Maybe . . . as your big boy runs off to play and the four-year-old snuggles against you for another story, somehow you realize that you have completely recharged. There is amazing power in a child's hug. It may be so much harder now that you have kids, but you'll take it over a quiet lunch at the bistro any day.

• • • • •

Juli Hiatt Caldwell is coauthor of the novel *Beyond Perfection*. She lives in Florida, where she spends her days as her children's chauffeur, volunteering at the school, writing, and trying to clean the cat hair off her couch.

Not Just Another Phase

By Dianna Graveman

"**C**an't she just forget about that for one day?"

It was Christmas time, and I was standing in line at a buffet-style meal in the midst of a large family gathering. My fourteen-year-old daughter, Teresa, was in line ahead of me, selecting vegetables and pasta from the array of dishes on display, but avoiding all of the meat. The comment from a well-meaning, but ill-informed (and dare I say insensitive?) dinner guest was just one of many my daughter and I had endured for the past three years, since Teresa became a vegetarian.

Many children enjoy spending time with animals, but Teresa's love for all living things had always carried an intensity that couldn't be denied. Her interest in other creatures took root in the earliest of her years, and she was forever bringing home hurt and homeless strays—a habit shared by her older brother and sister. We are a family of devout animal-lovers. But although the rest of us continued to include meat in our diets, Teresa's involvement and emotional connection with animals eventually led her to make a different choice.

I can't say Teresa's decision was an easy one for my husband and me to accept. She was only eleven when she announced herself a "vegetarian," and like everybody else, we assumed it was just a phase. It started one evening when she sat down to dinner and chose only vegetables for her plate, stating, "I am not going to eat meat anymore."

A few years later when Teresa was still not eating meat and it was clear this was not just another phase, we continued to encounter adults who dismissed her choice as temporary and frivolous. "A lot of kids go through that," we'd hear over and over. "She'll get over it."

Of course, I hadn't taken Teresa's decision about vegetarianism lightly. She was a child, and my first priority was her health, not her diet preferences. However, it was increasingly obvious that Teresa was not going to back down and start eating meat again. So we were off to the pediatrician for counsel as fast as we could get an appointment.

"There are things you need to be careful about," he told me, "but as long as she eats properly, she will likely be healthier than the rest of us."

After much research and further discussion with the doctor, Teresa and I agreed that she would pursue ovolacto vegetarianism, rather than something more drastic like veganism. This meant that she would continue to eat eggs, cheese, and other dairy products. Although a vegan's diet can be a very healthy one, I was a little nervous about leaping into so many changes at once.

My only concern was that she get what she needed nutritionally. Other adults had other concerns. Upon learning I had prepared a separate dish for my daughter's evening meal, a childless co-worker commented, "When I have kids, they'll eat what I put in front of them. I don't think it's right to spoil children that way."

People were forever expecting Teresa to "forget about it" if we attended a gathering where meat was served—as if a lifestyle choice can be "forgotten about" for a day.

It seems odd that our friends and relatives and colleagues couldn't forget about it instead. We never expected special considerations for Teresa. She ate whatever was available when we dined out, whether at somebody's home or at a restaurant. Teresa knew that she had made a decision that might not always be popular with others, and she was careful not to proselytize or expound on her ethics and motives unless she was asked to explain. And yet, if Teresa caught a particularly nasty virus or a bad cold, we were reminded that "maybe if she just ate a little more protein," this wouldn't happen. It was enough to make my husband and me question our support of Teresa's vegetarianism since everybody else seemed to. But Teresa is exceptionally strong-willed.

"What are we supposed to do, hold her down and force meat down her throat?" my husband asked angrily one evening after someone had made another hurtful comment about our inability to "control" our daughter.

What it came down to, finally, was this: We knew that we could support Teresa in this decision and help her make the

right nutritional choices– purchasing soy, tofu, and other products to supplement her diet—or we could oppose her, in which
case she would not eat the meat anyway and would run a risk
of health problems.

Teresa is sixteen now, and she has been a healthy vegetarian
for over five years. She is respectful of our diet choices, and we
are respectful of hers. She prepares her own meals when she
prefers not to eat what everyone else is having. Theresa's vegetarian lifestyle hasn't always been easy, but it has made us all
more sensitive to and tolerant of belief systems that differ from
our own. And I'm proud to say that Theresa has grown into a
strong and self-possessed young woman.

• • • • •

Dianna Graveman is a teacher and freelance writer. She has
a bachelor's degree in education and an M.F.A. degree in writing. She lives in St. Charles, Missouri, with her husband, three
almost-grown children, and a loveable mutt named Tramp.

Payback

BY REBECCA HOLDSWORTH

I was a much better parent five years ago, before I had children.

Before I had children, and especially in the period when I began thinking about having children, I blasted every perceived slip-up of every parent I saw. Leaving my house was no longer the innocent journey it once had been. I was watching and my mental checklist was working overtime.

See that mom with the screaming two-year-old in the men's section of the department store? If my child ever behaves that way I will pick him up immediately and march his little screaming self to the car.

And that "monster" in my favorite restaurant, screeching that she "wasn't going to eat that!" then crawling underneath the table not to be hauled out again until the check was signed and the tip left? My husband and I tsk-tsked. Our children will eat what they are given. They will use their utensils, speak in a properly modulated voice and always say "please" and "thank you."

The problem with today's children as I saw it was a lack of manners and respect. I saw this as a direct result of the "I'm OK, you're OK" parenting style so popular with some of my parents' generation.

What I didn't realize during those years of sticking my nose in the air and damning the bedraggled parenting masses was—someone was listening. And boy did I get my just due.

Do you remember that poor mother in the men's department store? The one stoically pushing her screaming toddler up and down the aisles of modern fashion? What I didn't realize between the wails for candy and shushes from Mom was if she went home without socks for her husband, she would have to tell him why he was missing all twelve pairs of work socks and why his sock drawer still held a residual smell of diaper cream. And right after the socks, Mommy had to buy more diaper cream—and put it up higher this time.

Remember that lovely couple with the child in the restaurant screeching about her meal? What I couldn't possibly have known while I was calmly munching on my appetizers and sipping on a cool glass of Chardonnay was that this family hadn't been out of the house in what seemed like an eternity. It was only their acute and unrelenting desire to eat somewhere where the meals didn't come in a folding paper box with a prize at the bottom that drove them to desperate measures.

What I didn't hear while enjoying light conversation about the state of the economy and our upcoming jaunt to the shore was their three-year-old swearing she would be good if she could just have a lobster like Mommy and Daddy. Only too eager for a quiet dinner, the parents took the bait. As the waitress set the glorious steaming delicacy under her little upturned nose the precious little angel began to shriek "I'm not eating that bug!" in a voice loud enough to rattle the windows.

I know all this because that was me and I was the one wanting to hide behind a clothes rack in the store and duck under the table in the restaurant.

It was also me who, while sitting in another restaurant talking to a friend while our children ate, heard a ripple of laughter pass through the dining room. I looked around to see what joke I was missing only to see my sweet and delicate daughter sitting demurely by with two French fries jammed up her nose. The joke was on me.

It was me who stood watching in the mall as my child threw herself onto the floor kicking and screaming after being denied another ice cream cone. It was me waiting in line at the upscale boutique while my little girl stood in the display window gaily waving and dancing for all the shoppers as they passed by. It was also me who turned to my friend and announced loudly and deceitfully so the cashier could hear, "Will you go and get your daughter!"

As for all of those things my husband and I swore we would or would not do? We have dragged the occasional child out of a mall for bad behavior but that was usually after the major purchase had been made and all bribery with lollipops had failed. Let's face it. How often can you find the time to even get to

the store much less find an opportunity to go again if you don't
get what you need? Where food is concerned, we do insist our
children try everything but you do have to admit a lobster "in-
the-rough" does look an awful lot like huge insect. A girlfriend
of mine recently confided she frequently roams the aisles of
her local grocery store trying to sing to herself loudly enough
to drown out the sound of her screaming toddler.

Parenting is a challenge. It is a joy, but it is a challenge. My
husband likes to repeat the adage, "The first casualty of com-
bat is the plan." In other words, nothing ever goes completely
to plan—not even parenting. Especially not parenting. You can
dream and wish and plan how you as a parent will handle your
future brood but until you are there in the trenches you will
never be sure. After all a family is the meshing of many different personalities in many different situations. Take two parents, one child, seven days in a week, fifty-two weeks in a year
(you can see where I am going with this)—and the possibilities
are endless.

I am not saying parenting should be likened to a battle
although some days it sure feels like one. It is actually the
opposite. In my case, being an effective parent is more about
not fighting. It is about choosing when and where and why I
want to "fight" and when to retreat.

I was a much better parent before I had children. Then
it was very simple. It was black and white. Yes and no. Then
again, maybe it wasn't. Maybe now that I am a parent I have
changed my definitions of what a good parent is. I know now

it isn't about appearances. They are going to scream. They are going to embarrass you. They are going to stick French fries up their noses. They are going to be . . . well, kids. The greatest tool we have in our parenting bag is a sense of humor.

As for anyone who feels a bout of judgment coming on as you witness some poor soul and his half-pint charges navigating through the mall or your favorite restaurant, be careful, especially if, say, you don't have kids yet or your kids are younger than the little hellions you're tsk-tsking. Any judgment you make may prove to come back to you. Remember: Someone is listening. He is taking notes and He has a sense of humor too.

• • • • •

Rebecca Holdsworth is a freelance writer and illustrator who has written on parenting issues for publications such as the *Boston Globe* and other parenting resources. Rebecca is also a pregnancy and newborn-parenting educator. She is the mother of two girls and two boys and lives in southern New Hampshire.

A Good Mother's Guide to the Sex Talk

By Micki Bare

Parenting, before I actually had children, seemed easy enough to my mind. I did not worry about deciphering different cries or diagnosing illnesses. I hardly gave a second thought to teaching my future children to walk or read. I never lost sleep over the prospect of teaching my future children to wash laundry, drive a car or balance a checkbook.

I guess I put a lot of faith in the experts. One trip to a mega-bookstore easily provides volumes of answers for parents. A couple of minutes on the Internet can also push away shadows of doubt, giving the most inexperienced parent-to-be unshakable confidence.

For the most part, when my children arrived and I began parenting for real, I did okay. If I was curious about something that was not clear in the hundreds of hours I spent reading the how-to's of parenting, I knew I could just ask an expert. As a result, I have clocked hundreds of hours talking to doctors and teachers. I bring a list of questions to every appointment or conference I've ever scheduled.

But as time wore on, a couple of looming parenting chores began to prey upon my mind. For starters, potty training terrified me. How in the world was I going to communicate to a child who had minimal verbal skills that using the bathroom facilities was preferable to wearing a diaper?

In the case of my diaper-versus-potty dilemma, my research paid off. I came across a list of ten things a child must be able to do before a parent should approach potty training. My children may have been almost three years old before I could check off all ten items, but it worked. To a young mother, the fact that I could train my children in only a couple of weeks bordered on miraculous.

Now, however, my children are approaching puberty. I always dreaded talking with my children about their changing bodies. Oh sure, health class at school covers the subject well. But good parents keep the lines of communication open. Good parents make sure their children will come to them with questions and concerns. Good parents are open and honest with their children about this life-changing, perfectly natural subject matter. At least, that is what I read.

However, as a young parent looking to the future, I could not picture myself having open, honest and perfectly natural conversations with my children. It was embarrassing enough when my parents openly and honestly conversed with me.

My parents talked with us before the health teacher separated the boys from the girls and showed those flowery filmstrips with pictures of puffy white clouds hovering over plush fields of green. I can still remember sitting on the floor in the dark watching the filmstrip thinking, "What does horticulture have to do with puberty?" Then it would hit me, "Oh no! Mom is going to want to talk about this when I get home!"

My very good parents, in their efforts to ensure that my siblings and I were well informed, took every available opportunity to discuss the "topic." And I in turn took every opportunity I could to avoid the "topic." As soon as my mother wanted to elaborate on the birds and the bees, I suddenly remembered a school project that was nearly due. My changing body was not something I wanted to discuss. Well, not with my parents, anyway.

As my children blissfully drifted through childhood, the impending "topic" began causing me anxiety once more. Only a few short memories ago, my children enjoyed running down the hall completely naked and dripping wet after bath time. But the moment they stopped asking for help changing clothes before bedtime, I could feel the "topic" weighing heavily on my shoulders. If I was too embarrassed to discuss this perfectly natural subject matter with my own very good parents, how was I going to be a very good parent myself?

I lost sleep worrying about handling the "topic" as my oldest finished up that last year of elementary school. Before sending children to middle school, our school system covers many aspects of the "topic," with parental permission, of course. When my son presented me with the flyer describing the impending "special" health class along with a permission slip, I knew it was time to start talking.

And yet as I went to begin, to my surprise I found that simple conversations about how a body changes or how boys and girls are different rolled right off the tongue. Maybe I'd underestimated how much my own experience pushing a child into the world with a roomful of relatives looking on could change my sense of what's embarrassing. Or maybe years of scrubbing poop out of cute baby clothing and wiping mucus off perfect button noses helped create special connections with my offspring that enabled me to freely and openly communicate about absolutely anything. It's also quite possible that my brain was so tired of cutesy baby talk by the time my oldest hit the fifth grade that any topic would have easily rolled off the tongue.

I may never know what got me started, but the key to keeping the lines of communication about the "topic" open has everything to do with the way my children reacted to my opening speech on puberty. I quickly discovered that my children are very easily embarrassed by the "topic." And I have to admit that it is really fun watching them cringe and squirm as I nonchalantly discuss the "topic" as easily as if I were discussing the latest pocket video gaming system.

Now that two of my three children have completed the public-school health class on the "topic," they've learned that once the door to the "topic" is even slightly ajar, Mom is going to facilitate an in-depth conversation about growing up. Every time I insist that we sit and review materials from health class, my children run and hide. Every time we watch something on television that opens the door for a new discussion on the "topic," my children change the channel to Cartoon Network. Then they inform me that the subject matter on the previous channel was inappropriate for young children.

But since I now know they'll run once I start freely and openly communicating, I simply save my growing-up lectures for road trips when I have a captive, properly restrained audience.

I never thought it would be possible. But I have to admit that now that I have children on the brink of becoming young men, I am having a lot of fun being a very good parent.

• • • • •

Micki Bare, a nonprofit director and freelance writer, calls on her experiences as a wife, mother, and professional to write a column distributed by the Arkansas News Bureau to Stephens Media newspapers nationwide. Her debut book, *Relative Expressions*, is available at *www.brandnewdaypublishing.com*. Micki and her family reside in Asheboro, North Carolina.

Baseball Pariah

BY LAURIE DIBERARDINO

As a child of European parents, I had no say-so. They decided what was best, how and when to handle situations, and also how to structure my life. They never asked me how their decisions impacted my life. Most often, they were wrong. So wrong.

I vowed to raise my son differently.

So I listened to Jake. I let him choose which clothes he wanted to wear, even if they didn't match. Dinner vegetables were a toss-up for him to decide. "Do you want cheese on top of the ham, or the ham on top of the cheese in your sandwich?" I would ask.

Okay. Maybe I went overboard at times. The point is: I was trying to teach him how to have his own voice, to be heard, so that he really *got* that his opinion mattered.

At the same time, I want to lead Jake in productive directions. As the sole caretaker and single mom of a five-year-old boy, I often check to make sure he is well-rounded, i.e., doing "boy" things, as well as the artsy activities that come more naturally to me. Jake's father, unfortunately, is not the let's-toss-a-ball-around type, although he is gifted with natural athletic ability, which my son inherited. Jake possesses a sinewy body coupled with superior strength that seems to amaze family, friends, and pediatricians alike. He has ranked in the ninety-fifth percentile or higher for height and weight continually since birth. However, he doesn't possess the confidence to carry that body with ease and doesn't seem to be internally comfortable with his strength and size. At five, he hasn't grown into his own body yet.

Flipping through our Park District guide, a summer T-ball class got my attention. I had heard my entire life from male friends, boyfriends, grocery-store clerks and men of all ages that if I ever had a son, to sign him up for baseball, that he would learn camaraderie, sportsmanship, and teamwork. The timing was good. He had just completed a Science for Small Hands class. He worked the brain, now it was time for the body.

I prepped Jake weeks in advance. Told him how he'd be meeting new friends, how lucky he was. We bought "cool" gym shoes. He seemed totally up for it. We exited the car fine with baseball glove and hat intact.

Within fifty feet of the ball field, his panic emerged, slowly unraveling like a spring bud.

My arm pulled and retracted like a taut rubber band. I turned and saw my slight son holding me back with determined dug-in heels.

"I don't want to go, Mom."

• •

That tiny voice trailing up to me and dissolving into the air like a vapor—how could I resist?

I attempted to talk him down as I stealthily uprooted him bit by bit. "Mom, don't make me go," he implored, his tears streaked with the dirt that always seems to be under little boys' fingernails.

So I let him choose to sit this one out, and Jake and I spent the first class teetering on a concrete-slab bench rooting for the other kids. After all, I did want him to enjoy this experience.

But I hoped he would play the second time. Jake began to resist the moment I let him know we had baseball class that day. He whined. He asked for seconds and thirds for breakfast. His stomach hurt. His legs "wouldn't work."

I lovingly reassured him. I validated his feelings. I let him know that I also was scared as a child when I had to try something new.

But I insisted. Perhaps I was overcompensating for the lack of a male role model in our household, but it seemed crucial to get him onto that ball field, and I was sure he would like it if he just gave it a chance. I maneuvered him into the back seat and slammed the door as he protested.

That session, he didn't start crying until we saw the ball field. I spent half of the forty-five-minute session attempting to get him to play in the game and the other half, he "played" half-heartedly.

I was determined week number three would be pivotal to both his child development and mine as a parent. If he didn't make it to the field for the entire session, I would refuse to go again. It was pointless. It was embarrassing in front of the other moms. I wanted to be one of the happy moms with their water bottles happily cheering for their own future Sammy Sosa.

These women at first gave me sad looks of support as I struggled with Jake to get on the field and have fun. Then the looks darkened to those of alarm and judgment. Finally, they stopped talking to me altogether.

I had turned into a baseball pariah.

That third day Jake was whining, crying, begging, and pleading not to go. His list of maladies grew: his legs wouldn't move, his back hurt, his eyeballs ached.

I could see that "good" mom wasn't cutting it. So instead of being the nice mom, the mom who offered treats if he played, the mom who said she would be proud as long as he tried—I became a shrew. With good intentions.

I barked that he had to play because "I said so." I spat out that I was disappointed that he didn't try, that he embarrassed me. Then I said that I didn't want him on the field, that he didn't deserve to play baseball. I stormed off, ordering him to follow me to the car.

My impersonation of a drill sergeant lasted only seconds. Although my son couldn't tell from my body language, inside I was churning in pain. How could I do this? What did I do to his psyche? Did I make a mistake that was irreversible and could never be corrected? Had I thrown four years of attachment parenting down the toilet?

I don't know. I never really thought about it much after that. Because my son stopped me from marching to the parking lot and rescued me from second-guessing my parenting skills. At least this time. He composed himself and said, "C'mon Mom, let me play."

I melted quickly. I fell to my knees, got really close, and buttressed his shoulders. "Are you sure? Are you really sure?" I asked.

With that, he pulled his cap over his chestnut eyes and trotted to the playing field. After that session, he went to the remainder of the baseball classes willingly and even admitted to enjoying himself.

As I watched him round the bases during the last game of the season, I breathed a sigh of relief. Whew. I made it through this one. What about next time?

• • • • •

Laurie DiBerardino, a Chicago native, has either written for, or edited magazines, books, and newspapers for thirteen years plus. Currently, she edits an international magazine catering to the cosmetic chemist. She serves as the eye of the hurricane in her life of raising one child, Jacob, amid the chaos of two dogs, two fish, and a cat.

The Barbie Ban

BY ANNE CALODICH FONE

Even before she was born, I had decided my daughter would not have a Barbie. I had read reports describing the unattainable image they were projecting to young, impressionable girls in our society. I knew that the older she got, the more my daughter would be bombarded with air-brushed pictures and ad-agency messages telling her that her mission in life was to have the right figure and find the right makeup and clothes in order to be happy. I might not have much control over those things later but I could certainly keep Barbie dolls away from her now.

Katie was nearing age five when she asked for her first Barbie. She had seen them and played with them, it turned out, at the homes of her friends. She was now telling me that what she wanted *most* for her upcoming birthday was "My First Barbie."

I stood my ground and did not give in to tears and pleas. I picked out and wrapped fun and educational toys as her presents, and when friends and family asked what Katie would like for her birthday, I left Barbie off the list. I was sure of what I believed.

When the day came, her birthday party was going smoothly and everyone seemed to be having fun. I had forgotten about the Barbie. But as both parents and children sat in a circle watching, Katie opened present after present of different Barbie dolls and outfits. What were these parents thinking purchasing such presents for such little girls anyway? I would have to exchange them for some other toys she liked when the celebration was over, I thought, convinced as I was that Katie had forgotten about Barbie.

But, before I knew it, pink boxes were all ripped into and destroyed as little hands grabbed everywhere and dressed and re-dressed these new additions to our family. They could no longer be returned. Well, she'll grow tired of them in a few days, I thought, as I cleaned up after the party and Katie sat mesmerized by her stash. But, day after day, she came home after school and rushed for the Barbies first.

I'll just quietly remove them and she won't even realize, I thought, after a few more days. I was wrong. And the fuss was loud and ugly. She did not understand. My husband did not understand either. "What is the big deal?" he asked. "But, they are *mine*!" Katie insisted. I admit it. I caved. I gave in. I let her keep and play with them.

I felt like I was letting my daughter down—and all little girls everywhere. Now that I'd relented, I tortured myself looking for one good reason to keep them.

To ease the torment, I decided to play with them with her. Get right down on the floor and play with those Barbies like I did with all her other unoffensive toys. At least, I could give her some direction as we played. We talked of different occupations and careers as depicted by some of the outfits. Okay, one was dressed as a doctor. Nothing wrong with that. We talked about how the clothes were pretty but how not everyone has fancy clothes—like at the shelter where we both volunteered. I felt the tiniest bit better but still, it all nagged at me, especially when I lay in bed at night.

Time passed and Katie still played with her Barbies almost every single day. Even when she was sick in bed, she would ask for them. A few more birthdays came and went and Ken and Skipper joined her family of dolls. It all felt so out of my control but I vowed at least to never buy one for her myself.

I didn't feel comfortable with Katie's doll collection until she was eight years old and her Barbies had been with us for three years. She had become fascinated with Broadway musicals and learned the scores to many shows. Standing silently outside her room one afternoon, I watched in amazement as she acted out scenes from *Annie*, *Bye Bye Birdie*, and *Joseph and the Amazing Technicolor Dreamcoat* with her entire cast of Barbie dolls.

The tug at my conscience finally eased. These were no longer the Barbies I feared but wonderful characters in and props for her active young imagination. In days to come, they would also become students in the imaginary classroom she taught in her room as well as ballet dancers in *The Nutcracker*.

Later, when Katie began taking ballet lessons and participating in dance recitals, I found myself unselfconsciously carrying a Barbie complete with tutu up to the cash register and home to her heart. Somehow, it just seemed natural now.

What I had feared most had not happened. Between my attempts at re-direction and her own imagination, Barbie had come to give my daughter many hours of pleasure and exploration into her own emerging interests.

Today, Katie is twenty-three. She still has a love of all things Broadway. We have enjoyed seeing many plays together and she has had the wonderful opportunity of acting in local theater productions of *Annie, Bye Bye Birdie,* and *Gypsy* as well as others. In high school, she played around with the idea of becoming a doctor but after working as a camp counselor, decided she could help children more by becoming a teacher.

As I write this, she is preparing for her first year teaching un-imaginary students in a school in rural Louisiana through Teach for America, just the way she did her Barbie dolls on the floor of her bedroom so many years ago.

Where are the Barbies now? Stored safely up in our attic waiting for the day Katie may have her own daughter with some fascinating interests and dreams of her own.

● ● ● ● ●

Anne Calodich Fone is a freelance writer whose purpose is to encourage others through her writing. She lives in upstate New York with her husband and best friend, Larry. Although her work has been published with over twenty companies, the creation she feels most proud of is her daughter, Katie.

The Resurrection of Bert the Goldfish

By Debby Simon

My soon-to-be five-year-old son, Benjy, was picking out his clothes for the day. It was almost time to leave for preschool. As he pulled his outfit from his dresser, he glanced at the fishbowl located on top where his two goldfish, Bert and Ernie, lived.

"Mom!" he shouted, "Come quick!" I hurried to his bedroom.

"Mom, look at Bert! He's lying on his side on top of the water. He's never done that before!"

I peered into the fishbowl. The brighter of the two goldfish was, indeed, lying on his left side, his right fin pointed toward the ceiling, his body arched in an uncomfortable pose. We watched in silence. Suddenly, the doomed fish fluttered, startling us.

"What's wrong with him?" I looked into my son's large brown eyes that were filled with concern. "Mommy, is Bert going to die?"

I watched him trying to grasp this unknown concept. Death was something he had not had to face in his young years. His eyes welled. How could he know or understand the concept of death already, how did he know that Bert was dying?

I was pregnant with our second child, already huge, suffering from sciatica, limited sleep, and constant trips to the bathroom since the baby's favorite position continually pressed on my bladder. My husband, who would have handled this far better than I, was out of town on business. I just couldn't bring myself to confront the issues of a dying fish, what death means, or the sadness that would follow on this particular morning.

I had never lied to my son before, but dishonesty began to flow from my lips and escalate with the grace and speed of a pole-vaulter.

"Oh, no, honey, Bert's not going to die, he probably just ate too much. He looks like he has a stomachache. How about, after I take you to preschool, if he isn't better, I'll call the vet."

"Can you take him to the vet?" he pleaded. Did he sense that I was lying? Would I have to explain about lying and death now? I had put myself in a difficult place by speaking before I thought.

Instead, I jumped into action because I realized that, if I didn't get my son out of his bedroom and off to preschool, I'd be caught. "We'd better get going, or you'll be late!"

"Mommy, will you take him to the vet right away?"

"Sure," I answered. How had I turned into a complete liar in a mere six minutes? The intensity of his concern and my sudden ease with lying made my heart ache. I dropped him off at preschool and returned home only to confirm that Bert had passed on.

I had to think. I grabbed a thick Ziploc baggy from the kitchen. I reached for the green fishnet and swept the dead fish out of the bowl and into the baggy. I didn't know if dead goldfish turn white or get pale, but I hoped that a little water might prevent a color change. I figured a little bit of water might be in order, so I held the baggy under the spigot. I then cleaned out the fishbowl so that Ernie wouldn't get sick. I refilled the bowl with dechlorinated water.

My mind was racing, plotting the rest of my dishonest scheme. My personal ethics and formerly honest relationship with my child had deteriorated in one morning, all over a dead goldfish. I rationalized that it was because my son couldn't handle the concept of death, and that this was really for his own good. But somewhere, from the depths of my parenting soul, I knew that I was the one who was afraid.

"Can I help you?" the clerk at the pet store asked. "Yes," I thought to myself, "Come over to my house and explain the concept of death and loss to my innocent son, who, in a few short months, will cease knowing life as it has existed when he is no longer an only child. And help me get him to forgive me for lying to him and then help me get rid of my guilt for the lies and deceitfulness that I am further perpetuating by patronizing your store."

"Yes, I need to find a goldfish," I said. "One that looks just like this one." I held up the Ziploc bag containing Bert. The clerk clearly did not comprehend. In fact, she looked somewhat grossed out.

"It's my son's pet," I tried to explain, smiling. "Well, he was my son's pet, and he's only four and a half." I paused, but the clerk was still staring at me with a blank look. "Oh, not the goldfish, my son," I elaborated. "My son is four and a half."

She still seemed bewildered, but she led me, waddling with my big belly, over to the aquarium tank that housed the store's supply of goldfish.

I peered inside. There were hundreds; how hard would it be to find one that looked exactly like Bert? "We've got a big selection. You want to look a bit and pick one out?"

Sure. I couldn't think of anything else I'd *rather* be doing! Doesn't *everyone* who enters a pet store and smells its distinct odors with a nose made stronger by pregnancy hormones want to linger as long as possible at 9:30 in the morning?

"Excuse me," the clerk said. "I'm going to help another customer and I'll be right back."

My pregnancy had not only enhanced my sense of smell, but had also made all of my senses keener. The clerk who had said she was going to help another customer was nearby. Though I know she didn't intend it, I clearly heard every word she was saying.

"Oh, *man,* have I got me a *winner!*" I heard her whisper. "You gotta check this one out! I've got some weird pregnant lady over there with a dead goldfish in a baggy! She's trying to find an identical match to the dead fish!" I heard snickering.

I crouched down (as much as I could) and, as silently as possible, stepped around the corner of the aisle. She was talking to the store manager!

"I hope you've finished with your other customer. I think I've found the right one," I said. She looked at me, back at the store manager, and then back at me. I could feel them fighting their overwhelming urge to laugh out loud.

"Great!" she offered. The store manager cleared his throat. The clerk followed me back to the goldfish tank and grabbed a plastic-lined Chinese-food-like takeout box that already contained water.

She netted the one I had selected after a few tries, dropped it into the waiting box and carried it to the register.

"Would you mind putting this in your trash?" I asked, trying to hand her the baggy with Bert #1.

"Uh, ma'am, we're not allowed to dispose of customers' dead animals," she said.

So I drove home with Bert the original and Bert the imposter. As I started to put Bert #2 into his new home, I suddenly had an awful thought. What if Ernie didn't like the new Bert? What if they started fighting? Do goldfish fight? What if Bert #2 could beat up Ernie and what if Ernie now died? Why hadn't I thought to ask about this at the pet store? Where was this new life of deceitfulness leading me?

"Ernie, meet the new Bert," I said, finally taking the leap. I gently put the new Bert into the fishbowl. I watched for a few minutes and breathed a sigh of relief. Bert #2 and the original Ernie looked just like before, swimming independently as well as swimming by each other, around, up and down in the large fishbowl.

I put my hands on my expanding hips and arched my back to stretch. I was feeling quite proud of myself. I had escaped uncomfortable issues. What had started as a simple lie had evolved into a highly detailed scheme and at that particular moment, my sense of relief outweighed my guilt and remorse. I smiled. My moment of criminal glory was interrupted by my sudden recollection that I had not gotten rid of the evidence.

"Oh *Lord*," I thought, and hurried down the stairs to retrieve the Ziploc baggy containing the original, dead Bert that was still inside my car. I felt a smidgeon of sadness as I flushed the poor fish down the toilet, then put the baggy into the trash.

When I picked my son up from preschool, he was happy and chattering about his day, never once mentioning Bert (#1).

" . . . and some kids got in trouble because they started calling Davey Jacobsen booger boy because he was picking his nose and eating it," he told me, laughing out loud. I smiled, and glanced at him sitting innocently in the backseat in my rearview mirror. My smile felt hollow. I was apprehensive and guilty.

I pulled into the garage. Before I could even maneuver myself out of the car seatbelt, Benjy bolted from the car and ran inside, flying up the stairs to his room. I trudged up the stairs after him.

He had a strange look on his face. "Where's Bert?" he asked.

BUSTED! If ever I needed a poker face, now was the time.

"What do you mean, Benj?" How were these words coming out of my mouth? Who was I? Did I need an exorcist? Why and how was I continuing to lie without even thinking about it? What kind of example was I setting for my son? How would he ever be able to trust me again?

"Where's Bert?" he asked, though he already knew. There was pain on his face.

"Where'd you get this fish?" The pain intensified because he had already figured things out, instinctively knowing that Bert was gone and, on some level, that I had not been honest with him. While he may not have figured out precise details, he certainly understood the big picture. He looked up at me, waiting for my explanation. "Tell me," he said, his voice quivering.

My heart sank. His innocent face was waiting for my explanation. How would I ever be able to amend my actions?

"Let's sit down on your bed," I began. I was relieved that he let me put my arm around him. "You know," I said, "you've had Bert and Ernie ever since you were two. Did you know that goldfish usually only live for a year to two years? You've had your goldfish for almost three years." Benjy looked up at me, his fear now confirmed. Huge tears rolled down his cheeks.

"I didn't want you to feel sad," I tried to explain. "When I got home from taking you to preschool, Bert had died." I paused. "I figured that Ernie would need a pal, so he wouldn't get lonely, and that you would still want to have two fish, and this fish looked just like Bert, so I bought a new fish." I was struggling to explain my actions now. Somehow, the image of Bert #1 fluttering, struggling, that morning seemed like a perfect metaphor for how I was feeling at this moment.

"Where is Bert now?" my son asked.

• •

Oh, no! How was I going to explain that he had been flushed to "goldfish heaven" via the city sewage system?

"Well, I imagine that Bert is in goldfish heaven."

"Is goldfish heaven the same as heaven?" he asked.

Wow. These concepts are hard enough for an adult to grasp.

"Well, yes, I suppose so," I said. "Death and heaven are hard things for us to understand, but I'm sure that Bert is happy now, and we should be happy to know he isn't in any pain," I said.

We sat on his bed for a long time. He asked poignant questions and I did my best to answer, as honestly as possible, with what I hoped was age-appropriate information. And I apologized. I told him how sorry I was that I hadn't been straightforward. I told him that I did not want to make him feel sad. And I promised that I would always tell him the truth from now on, even if the truth would make him feel sad.

After a long time, Benjy looked up at me. "Thanks for getting Ernie a new friend," he said. I breathed a sigh of relief. I had been forgiven. I hugged my son for a long time. This time the tears were from my eyes.

• • • • •

Debby Simon (aka "Mom" to Benjy, Alex, and Jorie) is a marcom professional with extensive experience in business writing, conceptual design, creative directing, and organizing carpools. She and her husband, Bob, enjoy music, reading, traveling, hiking, theater, and bragging about their kids.

Do You Have to Go to Work Today?

By Laura Allison Smith

J ust about every morning, when I take a quick break from dashing around the house putting away dishes and feeding the dog and making breakfast and wiping the countertops down—usually all at once, I wake up my sons and they almost immediately ask me, "Do you have to go to work today?"

This never fails to break my heart. I love my sons dearly, and have rearranged my life to make me a good mom and a better person. But the one thing I haven't been able to do—this from a woman who can make phone calls, do the dishes, referee a fight between two light-saber-wielding boys—is manage to be a stay-at-home mom.

Truth be told, I don't hate my job. Most days, that is. It's a decent job, pays pretty well, and gives me the freedom to have lunch with my kids relatively often.

But there's a downside. A list of the things I did yesterday:

Made breakfast for family,
Drove to work,

Wrote three articles and arranged for several interviews,
Took the dog to the vet,
Went grocery shopping,
Unloaded groceries,
Cleaned dried up apple juice off of walls and leather
    furniture,
Mopped floors in kitchen and two bathrooms,
Took the boys to swim lessons,
Made dinner,
Made flight plans for a trip to Disney World,
Helped the boys drag action figure from the bottom of a
    muddy culvert near house (unsuccessfully),
Bathed the boys,
Put the boys to bed (8:30 P.M.), and
Entered two-months' financial info into Quicken.

Seriously. Working full-time, it's impossible not to be so thoroughly stretched, so insanely scheduled, that I feel exhausted at the end of the day just *thinking* about all the things I manage to get done. I am routinely amazed at my ability to multitask. I look at that list now and wonder how I did it. How I managed to spend any "quality time" with them. I wonder if I did, in all that rushing around. Why do I want to be such a perfectionist?

The bitter answer to that question, of course, is that I don't want my boys to suffer because I work full-time. I want to do all the things that stay-at-home moms do so effortlessly. To go to the park, swim, have long play groups, and bring casseroles to new moms. Which is all stuff I schedule into my already-overscheduled weekends, to make me feel less guilty.

When *Time* magazine published a cover story about the resurgence of at-home mothering and about how important having a stay-at-home mom is, it all made me want to crawl into a hole and die. I got the distinct sense that I might as well start saving to bail my neglected kids out of jail when they're adults. Because the truth is, I would give almost anything to stay at home with my kids. But I can't. My family needs the money.

Here's another truth: as much as I envy stay-at-home moms, I hate them. I resent that they are so often snide and self-righteous about their ability to be at home, the long hours they're able to put in at the park and make cookies *all in one day,* the freedom they have to work their schedules around their children's schedules.

Okay, so maybe some of this is my defense mechanism coming on. But the luxury of it all! What I would give to complain about cleaning all day or getting sunburned at the park from flying kites all day! These at-home moms scrapbook, for God's sake, and they do things like make picture frames out of aluminum cans and dental floss. Would I do any of these crafty things were I a stay-at-home-mom? No possible way. But I can almost salivate thinking about how comfortable my life would be if I didn't have to go to Wal-Mart to buy diapers at 10:00 P.M. with sweatpants on over my nightgown because I couldn't get to it earlier.

I make a conscious effort to be happy in the life I have, as busy as it is. And for the most part, I am indeed happy. I have a husband who loves me and two healthy, happy kids, a comfortable home, and a dog. Which, by the way, needs to go back the vet. Which needs to be scheduled, along with a well-child visit to the pediatrician and a long-neglected appointment to get my hair colored. Because it's getting grayer by the day.

• • • • •

Laura Allison Smith is the wife of Chris Smith and the mother of Harrison and Del. She can be found at her home in Paradise, California, simultaneously climbing trees and baking cookies.

Bedtime

By Elana Zaiman

"Is there anything you enjoy doing with him?" Anita asked when I picked up Gabriel at day care this afternoon. Anita is a short woman with salt-and-pepper hair, hazel eyes, and a mango-shaped body. She stared at me with questioning eyes, upturned brows, and a skewed upper lip. Was it because I expressed dismay that her day care would be closed for a few days? Because I complained I needed more hours in my day? Because I was annoyed Gabriel was acting his age? I'm not sure.

Her words stung.

Anything I enjoy doing with him? Doesn't she see how he smiles at me when I walk in the door of her day care? Even his large gray-blue eyes smile. Surely she sees how he runs toward me screaming, "Mommy, Mommy, Ma," his blond curls bouncing as he runs. True, there are times he ignores me. Times he yells at me when I try to put on his jacket. "Mommy. Mommy. Go away, Mommy." But within moments he wants to be held. Aren't most two-year-olds like miniature adolescents?

At 7:45 P.M., I bathe Gabriel, wash his hair, brush his teeth, and dress him for bed. He wears his winter gray sleep suit with the royal blue neck and cuffs that highlight his gray-blue eyes. His blond wet curls I cannot bear to cut hang down past his neck. I ruffle his hair, kiss his soft Dove-scented cheeks, let him nestle into my body.

"Mama, read," he says. He hands me a book.

It's 8:30 P.M. We are sitting in Mommy and Daddy's bed with a pile of bedtime stories: *Curious George Feeds the Animals*, *Blueberries for Sal*, *Maisy Makes Gingerbread*, *Maisy Takes a Bath*, and *Murmel, Murmel, Murmel*.

"Maisy. Let's read about Maisy and Tallulah in the bathtub," I say.

"Maime," he says.

Anything I enjoy doing with him? "Sure," I said. "I enjoy doing lots of things with him." She didn't believe me.

What mother enjoys being with her two-year-old twenty-four hours a day? I admit I don't. I need time alone. Time to read. To write. To think. To be. With no time to myself I'd lose it.

When Gabriel's not at day care, I'm with him. Except when I have to cook dinner, fold laundry, answer the phone, return calls. I guess I don't have to answer the phone when it rings, or return people's calls when he and I are playing with Legos, blocks, or puzzles. Many times I don't. Sometimes I do.

"Boogers," he says. He sticks his fingers up my nose.

"No boogers," I say. "Honey, please take your fingers out of my nose."

Anita's questioning my desire to be a mother. She senses motherhood is just a job. Sometimes I think she worries about me, about Gabriel. I think she wonders to herself: "How can you even think of having another child?" I've told her I'm considering it. We talk a lot when I pick Gabriel up at 4:00 in the afternoon. I learn a lot from her. She keeps me sane. At least, I thought she did.

I'm a fine mother, I want to tell her. Besides, I pay you for day care, not to comment on my mothering. I judge myself enough. I don't need your help.

Just ask Gabriel, I want to say to her. Ask him if his mom enjoys spending time with him. He'll say "yes." If he had the words, he'd tell you how I dress up in his "blankey," and his hats, and perform skits for him when he's eating lunch. He'd say, "My mom makes up silly songs and funny dances. I giggle so hard I have to hold up my head so it doesn't fall into my food."

All experienced parents say; "These years pass so quickly. Cherish them." Sometimes, I cherish the moments. But not all moments are worthy of being cherished. Sometimes motherhood feels like a job, especially on long cranky afternoons.

In just a few hours I've been remembering tons of stories to tell Anita so she won't think me unloving or inept. Like how I love to watch Gabriel scream "biggie swide," before he slides down the big slide in the park.

How I love to watch him join older children in their game of basketball by standing in the middle of the court, unaware he's in the way and will be knocked over.

How I love to watch him sidle up to a four-year-old girl he has never seen before, smile into her eyes, and mimic whatever she is doing.

How I love to watch him carry the police car, two fire-trucks, dump truck, helicopter, two boats, and bus, one at a time up the jungle-gym, and then one by one, push them down the slide, clapping and screaming in excitement when one by one they hit the earth.

How I love to watch him lie on our den floor, singing nonsense songs to himself, looking over at me every two minutes to make sure I'm listening.

I will tell her how much I enjoy reading with him, tickling him, and sharing Popsicles. "Mmm," he says. "Mommy, mmm," as the tangerine Popsicle juice drips down his chin.

I will tell her how he rubs my arm with his soft hands, says, "skin touch," and then hugs my arm tight like a stuffed animal. I'll tell her his zoo reports. "Peacot." "Beaw." "Nake."

I wish Anita could see us now as we sit on Mommy and Daddy's king-size bed for story time. I wish she could see him look up at me with his large gray-blue eyes, bat his long blond eyelashes, smile, lean his body into mine.

"Eyebwow," he says. He traces my brown eyebrows with his right pointer finger.

"Yes, honey, you're right. That's my eyebrow."

"Bwail, eyebwow?" he asks.

"Yes, Gabriel has eyebrows too," I say. His eyebrows are so blond they are hard to detect.

• •

"Yah." He claps his hands together and smiles.

Maybe I shouldn't confide in her anymore. Days when I pick him up early I vent my frustrations. I find it hard to balance my life. Being a mom. Serving as part-time rabbi/chaplain at an old age home. Teaching. Counseling. Keeping house. Doing errands. Writing. Taking writing classes. Studying with my writing mentor.

I tell Anita I'm writing, a dream of mine for years. I tell her how hard it is to get the words to come out on paper, to believe in myself as a writer. I figured Anita would appreciate my attempt to balance my life. After all, she's a mother of three. Two in college, one in elementary school. Surely she can remember what it was like when her kids were young. Lack of sleep. Temper tantrums. She's told me on occasion she would lock her kids in their rooms until they left their tantrums behind and were ready to join the family again. I thought she understood. I didn't think she'd use my words against me, throw my struggles back in my face as we stood in the middle of the day-care floor.

Maybe it's true that we only understand something when we live it. A mother of toddlers only understands what it's like to parent toddlers. A mother of teenagers only understands what it's like to parent teenagers. Ask a mother of teenagers about toddlers. She won't remember.

"Mommy, bearwt?" Gabriel asks. His soft little fingers graze my cheek and chin.

"No, honey, Mommy doesn't have a beard. Mommy has soft skin."

. . . .

"Daddy, bearwt?"

"Yes, honey, at the end of the day, daddy has a beard."

"Gabiel, bearwt?"

"No, honey, Gabriel doesn't have a beard yet."

"Mommy, man?" he asks.

"No, Mommy's not a man. She's a woman."

"Mommy, woman. Daddy, woman?"

"No, Daddy's a man."

"Daddy, man. Bwail, man?"

"Gabriel will be a man someday. Right now Gabriel's a boy."

"Bwail, boy. Man."

Maybe I should apply for a full-time rabbinical job in the Jewish community, earn a full-time salary. Then I wouldn't have to feel guilty placing him in day care. No. I'd feel worse. Less time with him. No time to write. I want to write.

My mom never worked full-time when we were growing up. She taught a few hours a week in the afternoon Hebrew school at our synagogue. There were four of us. I can't imagine parenting four children. As to what my mother did when she was not spending time with us, not preparing for her classes, not teaching, not sewing, I'm not sure. I know she was not with us twenty-four hours a day.

I remember some of our babysitters when we were young; John, Dunny, HannaLee, Mrs. Conti, Marion, Mrs. Sayer, Helen, who I used to call "Hell" for short, unaware *hell* had another meaning. In my twenties, my mother told me a woman

• •

congregant from my father's synagogue walked by our house once when I called Helen, "Hell," and gave my mother an angry stare. "What did you do?" I asked. "Nothing," my mom said. "I figured it was her problem. It's not like you knew what it meant."

My mother was judged. All mothers are judged. Mothers judge one another. Mothers judge themselves.

In my early thirties, my mother told me that when we were old enough to look after ourselves, she would sometimes lock herself in the bathroom to read, to think, for peace and quiet. When first she told me, I was angry, hurt. I judged her. That was before I became a mother. Now, I understand. Sometimes, I go into the bathroom for privacy. Still I continue to judge my mother as this day-care provider judged me.

Anything I enjoy doing with him? Perhaps I complain about the toddler dance class and his clinginess, saying "uppy-duppy," crying, screaming, or kicking until I pick him up. Anita's in the dance class with four toddlers in her care. Out of the corner of her eye she must see how Gabriel works me. I imagine she thinks I'm not firm enough, that I should take charge.

Does she think I don't enjoy being with him because I can't contain my excitement when she tells me a child is moving out of town and three hours have opened up on Wednesday mornings? I'm thrilled. It's true. Not because I don't enjoy him but so I can write. After dance class, even on good days, I'm exhausted, and I find it hard to return to the quiet internal space the day has interrupted.

• •

I imagine she thinks I'm being selfish, wanting to write. I should wait until Gabriel is older. Now I'm a parent—the most important responsibility in the world. How can I entrust my child to anyone else?

"Don't you understand what would happen if I starved my soul, stopped my creative work?" I want to say to her. "I'd be no good for myself, or for Gabriel. I'm a better mother when my soul is fed."

Besides, how would she earn her livelihood if not for parents like me? No. She's not the enemy. I'm my worst enemy. I judge myself more critically than anyone could ever judge me. It's hard enough being a parent. I must be kinder to myself.

"More re-read," Gabriel says. He picks up a book we have already read.

"Honey, we've read five books already. Time to turn out the light, to talk about the day." My voice cracks.

"Mama, cwying."

"Yes, honey, Mommy's crying."

"Teaws," he says, and points to my tears, still visible in the hallway light.

I've cried three times since I picked him up at four o'clock. All because of her question. "Is there anything you enjoy doing with him?"

I can't take her offhand comment so personally. I have to remind myself that she told my husband and me on separate occasions, "It's great watching you two. You have so much fun with him."

"Cuddle," he says. We both lie down. Gabriel nuzzles into the crook of my arm, inches his body backward into mine. I hug him.

"Honey, what did you do today?" I ask him.

"Pway. Dump twuck. Cwane."

"Did you have a good day?"

"Yahhhhh."

"Let's talk about tomorrow," I say. "Tomorrow you go to school."

"Kool."

"Yes, school. Then we go to Mimi and Poppy's."

"Mimi. Poppy."

"It should be fun," I say. "Now who loves Gabriel?" I ask.

"Mimi and Poppy," he says. "Mommy and Daddy."

I mention his other grandparents Grammy and Zayde, his great grandma, aunts, uncles, and cousins by name.

"Who else loves Gabriel?" I ask.

"Michaew," he says. He means his best buddy, Michael. "Cindy," he says. She's Michael's mommy. Then he adds his babysitter, "Bubbie Wael," Lael, and his next door neighbor "Doughy," or Zoe.

"Does Gabriel love Gabriel?" I ask him.

"Yah," he says dutifully.

"Good," I say. "It's important for Gabriel to love Gabriel. Honey, it's time for Shema. Then I sing in Hebrew, "Shema Yisrael Adonai Elohenu Adonai Echad." "Hear, O Israel: The Lord our God, the Lord is One."

• •

I carry Gabriel into his room, and I bend down so his hand is even with the light switch and he can turn off his overhead light. He gives me a big neck hug before I place him in his crib.

"Chalomot paz, golden dreams," I say.

"Gowdin dweams," he responds.

"I love you."

"Wuv wu," he says. He lies on his tummy, puts his hands under his pillow, turns his head to the right, and looks up at me.

"Sleep well. I'll see you in the morning."

"Mawning."

"Night night," I say. I walk out of his room and close his door.

Is there anything I enjoy doing with him? No. Nothing. Nothing at all.

• • • • •

Elana Zaiman is a rabbi, teacher, chaplain, and writer. Her nonfiction and essays have appeared in *American Letters and Commentary, Calyx,* and other literary journals and anthologies. She lives in Seattle with her husband and son.

Cutting the Cord

By Nikki Katz

Always a perfectionist, I became obsessed with doing everything for Katelyn when she was born. I don't think my husband even held her during the first few hours after she was born. She was my baby and I was damned if I was going to let anybody screw her up. I showered her with love and attention, making sure to be the focal point in her tiny little world. I cringed when my friends and family played with her, using incorrect grammar or singing songs off-key. I just knew that this would affect Katelyn's future SAT scores and chances of getting into Princeton. Yes, she's going to Princeton. I didn't get in, so she's going to attend in my place.

Katelyn was a sheltered child, not very social, and she didn't react well when I tried to leave for an hour to do something for myself. I felt guilty every second I was away, even if she was just in the children's room at the gym (screaming her little head off for the ten minutes they allowed before paging me). Lucky for Katelyn, I had another baby when she was twenty months old. From the moment she was born, my relationship with Kendall was different. My labor was very fast, and very intense. I didn't even make it to the delivery room—I gave birth in the elevator. Although it was a liberating experience, especially as I was determined to have a natural delivery, I found that I didn't experience that immediate connection with her. I loved her and was excited to meet her, but I was not nearly as possessive as we moved to the delivery room and got checked in. Unlike when Katelyn was born, I was very comfortable with Kendall being passed among the family members. Perhaps it's because she was the second child, or perhaps it was because I did not develop the same expectations during my very long labor with Katelyn.

Kendall quickly developed pneumonia, most likely as a result of the rapid delivery. The doctors said she probably had residual fluid in her lungs that was not expelled as I pushed her out. They whisked her off to the NICU while I stayed in the delivery room with excessive bleeding. When I was finally able to go see her after my situation was stabilized, I was told she was going to have to remain in the hospital for a week. I began crying and shaking. My baby was going to have to stay in the hospital? I had just assumed she could go home with me the next day and we could start our future as a family of four.

After my initial shock, I began to worry about how to divide my time over the coming week, ultimately deciding that Kendall needed my time and attention more than Katelyn did. That week was a turning point in Katelyn's nurturing. I spent a good deal of each day at the hospital while my mother stayed home to help with Katelyn. And as much as I hate to say this, I'm not sure that Katelyn ever knew I was gone!

After Kendall came home from the hospital and my leash on Katelyn continued to loosen, I was amazed at how this loosening transformed my daughter. Katelyn began to interact more with others and wasn't so shy in social settings. She became animated and loved receiving attention from others. She's now a completely different child, at ease with the world.

Kendall has been like the new Katelyn from the beginning. I realized that I didn't need to encase my daughters in the glass cage I had created as a barrier between the world and us.

Although we shattered the cage, I still haven't been able to drop the neurotic need to do everything by myself. I'm a work-at-home-mom, and even when I have an extremely tight deadline, I find it hard to ask for help. I don't want to search out others to be a parent for me. That's *my* job, and it's one I better excel at! I fear what would happen to my psyche if I got somebody in here . . . a mother's helper, a nanny, a babysitter . . . call it what you want. What if Katelyn went to this "other woman" when she skinned her knee, instead of me? What if Kendall took her a book to read, instead of toddling into the office to climb in my lap? It would honestly break my heart. I had issues enough with Katelyn running to my mother-in-law instead of me when we both went to pick her up from preschool one day. I smiled, but inside I was seething. And there are often days when Katelyn doesn't want to come home from school at all.

I don't ever want to be accused of not being able to handle parenthood. I want to have it all—being a mommy, being a wife, being a writer, being a friend, keeping a nice home, and cooking a great meal. That also means being perfect at everything I do. I have this immense fear of being judged. But modern moms tend to do that. They judge their peers, their parenting styles, and their children's behavior. It's become a huge contest to see whose child can be the brightest, most talented, most beautiful, most social, most well-mannered, and most well-rounded. And then there's the media's contribution in the form of instructional books, educational videos, and infant enrichment classes.

I used to buy into the obsessive need to purchase every educational toy and product. But Katelyn refused to watch a single episode of Baby Einstein, and both girls would rather play with the remote control than their Leap Frog alphabet bus. So, what's a mom to do? I have all the toys upstairs in the loft, where we rarely hang out, and the remote control downstairs, sans batteries.

And I'm slowly beginning to ask for help. It's better than feeling guilty when I'm holed up in the office with a tight deadline and the girls are running circles around the television, or when, stretched by the demands I've made on myself, I lose my patience and my temper. Or when I check my e-mail for the twentieth time in one day instead of reading the book Kendall brings to me. So I've started off small, asking my mother-in-law to help out one afternoon a week. I know they're safe, and having a great time. They're also forming a relationship with their grandmother, which is invaluable. And I'm enjoying the peace and quiet while I focus on work. In fact, I'm expanding my horizons and looking for a mother's helper to assist on another afternoon.

I find that the time I spend away from my children helps in many ways. I give dedicated attention to my work for a set amount of time, and then I come home and give dedicated attention to the girls. I actually miss them when I'm working, instead of being aggravated that they're around.

Does this mean that I'll hire a nanny? I doubt it . . . but you never know!

• • • • •

Nikki Katz is a freelance writer and author on a variety of topics including women's issues, pregnancy, puzzles, and games. She has written four books, has been published in magazines, and maintains and writes for multiple Web sites. She can be reached via her personal Web site, *www.nikkikatz.com.*

Something Tells Me Too Much Happened at the Zoo

By Yvonne Piasecki—Teddy

My five-year-old daughter had a cold and fever over the weekend that extended to Monday, so I kept her home for the day. On Tuesday the fever had broken, so I sent her to school—and worried about it. She was very quiet and would not eat much breakfast. But I felt I could not justify another day off from school.

At the end of the day when I picked her up, she was sobbing, pale, and exhausted. I calmed her down and felt her forehead, and she felt feverish. Yet she had many exciting animal stories to tell me about.

We went to the doctor to get her ears checked for a possible infection. On the way there, she started her story again about what she learned that day about polar bears. When I asked if her teacher shared a new book with the class, she softly replied "No, I saw the bears at the zoo. Today was our field trip."

Field trip! I forgot about the field trip!

I felt so *guilty*!!!!!!!!!!!!!!! And when we discovered at the doctor's office that my daughter's temperature was almost 103 degrees, I was mortified. How could I have sent her to school, then on a field trip *outside* to the *zoo*?

The nurse tried to make me feel better. She reminded me that without a fever, the field trip would have been fine, and that the fever probably developed as the day progressed. How was I to have known?

Needless to say, I felt like a terrible mom. I know that this experience will not affect her life in the long-term sense, but it really prompted me to doubt my ability to "read the signs" of distress in my child. I felt guilty because I forgot about the trip, and the thought of her roaming from the indoor to the outdoor exhibits for five hours was difficult.

My husband seems immune from this level of concern. His response was: "So, she has a fever. Give her some Tylenol, the meds from the doctor, and put her to bed." It never seemed to upset him nearly as much as it upset me. It must be a "Mom" thing!

My daughter is feeling better, thanks to the antibiotics, bed rest, and lots of liquids. She will enjoy a quiet, restful weekend at home, sans polar bears. And I'll be checking her temperature every hour on the hour.

• • • • •

YVONNE PIASECKI-TEDDY is the mom of Jessie Rose, age six. She has been a middle-school teacher since 1991. Her interests include reading, writing, and travel. She currently lives in Wisconsin with her daughter and husband.

The First Cut

By Stephanie Viter

uilt. I'm a single parent, so I know it well. When my son was about a month old, I had become pretty good at changing diapers, feeding, and giving baths, but there was one thing I hadn't tried yet—cutting his fingernails.

It was time. At first, everything went well. The baby was happy, I was happy, and all was right with the world. Then the unthinkable happened. The phone rang and I was concentrating so hard that I jumped. The baby started to cry, first softly, then really hard. I looked down and noticed that I had accidentally cut his finger. Even worse, it was bleeding. Though it was only a drop or two, to me it looked like a river. I quickly grabbed a tissue and wrapped it around his little index finger. I went to the medicine cabinet and got the smallest Band-Aid I could find. I wrapped his finger up like a mummy, cursing the entire first-aid industry for not making baby-sized bandages, and myself, for cutting him in the first place.

That's when it began to hit me. Guilt. Shame. I had injured my child. Accidentally, but still he was hurt. I knew I was a bad

• •

mother. Tears began to well up in my eyes. My baby cradled in my arms, I did the only thing I could do at that point. I called my mother.

"What's wrong?" my mother asked, worriedly.

"You won't believe what I did, Mom."

"What did you do?"

"I was cutting Ben's fingernails and I accidentally cut his finger!" My voice collapsed into a heap of sobs.

"That's it?" she asked, taking a deep breath.

"Yeah. I'm the worst mother in the universe."

"No, honey, you're not. You're a good mom. Is he okay?" I could hear her starting to chuckle.

"He was crying pretty hard, but," I looked down and saw him lying happily in my arms. Finally, calm came over me. "I think he's okay now."

"Honey, he's fine. You're human. Things like this will happen. Just do the best you can. That's all you can do."

She was right. We aren't perfect. We just have to do the best we can and hope everything works out in the end. It really is all we can do.

• • • • •

Stephanie Viter lives in Iowa with her three-year-old son. She works in retail merchandising and writes mainly as a hobby. This is her first published story.

Cheap, Lazy Mother

By Leslie Fowler Doyle

When our children were born, my husband and I thought at first, "Anything these two cuties want, it's theirs." We purchased many expensive gadgets and toys, all new.

But time passed and we came to our senses. We had decided that I would stay at home and enjoy their many "firsts." So we took up yard-sailing, as we called it. As the weekend dawned, with bottles, stuffed bears, and Cheerios in tow, we headed for the yard sales.

These forays required planning and strategy of the highest level, much like a military operation. Early in the morning, I ran out to retrieve the newspaper, as my husband prepared breakfast. The children were still asleep. As I scoured the ads for the required items, he gathered the essentials for the morning's excursion. I mapped out the sales that we would attend and the route we would take, from most promising sale to least promising. Any seasoned yard-sale consumer knows where to go, to go early, and to have goals.

• •

At the last moment, we would scoop up the little angels and place them in their car seats, and the drive to the first sale would be the last blissful moments of rest we had all day. Then, off we would go, into the rising sun to hunt down and gather the weekend's plunder. Seeing the brand name "Little Tikes" in an ad, we were like the Spanish seeing the Aztec gold for the first time. I can distinctly remember our quest to buy a "Cozy Coupe." After repeated failures, we finally came to a yard sale, and off in the distance, about a half a block away, I spotted my treasure, but my husband couldn't park the car. "Jump out!" he yelled and I willingly complied. I bounded like a gazelle toward the little car, pulling my money out of my purse as I ran. I could see myself in slow motion as I strained the last few feet for the prize. "Sold!" I screamed as my hand touched the roof. At that moment, I felt the joy of a victorious Olympian.

Our children enjoyed yard sales, too, but in a different way. My husband and I found toys, books, games, and other items in good condition. Our children could always sniff out the broken part and missing pieces box and find their booty there. Many dolls were taken for the "orphanage" at our home and cars without wheels were valued beyond measure. Our daughter also found her first collection of Barbies. Our son zeroed in on his first monster truck.

As the children have grown, so have their number of outlets for energy and entertainment. However, I have an allergy to driving constantly and have an even deeper phobia to having more than several commitments a week. So, I have pleaded

• •

chronic fatigue and decided to limit their activities. Activities have a way of exponentially reproducing. It's not just the activity: it is the concessions, fundraising, practices, and unexpected extras that take you over the top. Before you know it, the week is gone and you barely know your husband and children. Knowing that one day our children will be permanently busy, we have opted to spend relaxed evenings with them, playing games and talking. Life moves too quickly not to enjoy them.

I have purposefully given them many empty days in summer without hope or prospect of movies or computer games so that they will summon their creativity. They have had to climb trees, swing on the play set, capture bugs, and ride their bikes. They have gone into several business enterprises. Separately, our daughter has ruled her kingdom like a fairy princess and our son has kept the world safe from fire with the rescue unit of which he is the commander. Together, they are the most conniving spies. They have even resorted to putting on shows. Out of sheer desperation, they made interesting inventions. Once, our daughter made an obstacle course for our son for his "soldier training." It was used by other future soldiers in the neighborhood. These quiet hours have also forced them to build tents and draw. An inside version of a sheet tent was made and its rooms were expanded into a yurt that Genghis Khan would envy. Of course, it was strategically placed so that moving around our home, from room to room, was out of the question.

And to think that none of this would have happened if I had had a little more money and energy.

• • • • •

Leslie Fowler Doyle is a wife, the home-schooling mom of two children, and personal zookeeper to the family goldfish and guinea pig. She has written for the *Journal of Family Ministry, Church Libraries Magazine* and *http://ChristianActivities.com.* She is currently a contributor to *KidznCommunities* magazine in Pittsburgh, Pennsylvania.

The Sick Sense

BY GWEN MORAN

'm standing in front of the mirror, trying to remember how to put on mascara without poking myself in the eye. On the bed, stockings and the one dress (black, of course) that makes me look like I have a waist are laid out. Earlier in the day, I went to the salon and had my hair blown out and my nails done. The reservations are made, and the babysitter's on her way. My husband and I are going out on a real date. And I'm as giddy as I was when he first asked me out more than ten years ago.

As I pluck the last stray eyebrow hair and survey the result of my rusty makeup skills in the mirror, my darling two-year-old shuffles into the bathroom. I look down at her lovingly, and my heart drops.

Glassy eyes. Flushed cheeks. She says the dreaded words that I already know, "Mommy, I don't feel good," and then throws up on my new pedicure.

I take her temperature (102.7 degrees) and weeks of planning break down with the efficiency of roadies breaking down the last night of a Springsteen show. Reservations and babysitter canceled. Dress and stockings back in the closet. My $35-plus-tip hairstyle is now pulled back in a clip, as my well-manicured hands are getting pruned from dipping a cloth into cold water to cool my daughter's forehead.

While you may not believe in ESP, or the so-called "Sixth Sense," there's little doubt that most children possess a different kind of supernatural power—the ability to know when their parents have planned a big night out and then spike a fever so high it can be used as an alternate source of home heating. I call it the "Sick Sense," and it's ruined more nights out than I can count.

There was the year we celebrated Christmas with pinkeye. The Easter party we had to leave early because of a sudden fever caused by an ear infection. And my husband and I have attended so many events solo, one of us staying home with our sick child (usually after losing several rounds of "Rock, Paper, Scissors"), that our friends are beginning to wonder if we've secretly split up.

The only way I've found to outwit the sick sense is to make last-minute plans that require minimal preparation and no fancy clothes. I've yet to deal with sudden illness when we've decided at the last minute to go out for pizza, especially if we're heading to Chuck E. Cheese.

So, this Valentine's Day, my husband and I have made our arrangements for a two-person-only night out with the stealth and precision of Navy Seals or CIA agents under deep cover. Our babysitter is secretly lined up. At the appointed time, we'll call her with a code word that means we'll be dropping off one female toddler within fifteen minutes.

Like plain-clothes detectives, we'll be dressed in our regular garb as we load our darling daughter into her car seat and hide her over-stuffed diaper bag in the trunk. Once the drop is made, we'll make our getaway, spending a romantic evening at the only place that can accommodate us without reservations on February 14—the parking lot of the local KFC, where we'll dine on Extra Crispy–style drumsticks and large Diet Cokes.

It'll be the healthiest holiday we've had in years.

• • • • •

Between swigs of Tylenol and Pepto-Bismol, **Gwen Moran** writes for magazines and book publishers. Her work has appeared in *Entrepreneur, USA Weekend, Woman's Day, Family Circle* and others. She is the coauthor of two books. Don't tell them, but she frequently recounts funny stories about her family at *www.gwenmoran.com*.

Just This Once

BY JOSÉE MALO

Quite significantly, it happened on a Monday. When I decided to go back to work part-time after the birth of my baby, I pictured my Mondays at home with my baby full of laughs, long walks, homemade cookies, story books, and finger painting. Dazzling moments, somewhere between a diaper commercial and the cover of a parenting magazine.

But the image had never really come into focus. After a year, it was still far from glossy. There we were, my sixteen-month-old and me: it was Monday. But there were no arts and crafts in sight. No aroma of freshly baked goodies. And the only sound one could hear for miles around was my heavy sighing. Providing the tyrant was not whining, of course.

It had been quite a morning. No food would pass those toddler lips. The loud "No!" that still sounded so cute yesterday was about to make me lose my mind. No airplanes, no cars, no trucks would open the little garage door. With all these vehicles in the kitchen, it had to end in a crash: everything found its way to the floor . . . to the golden retriever's delight.

I admit that I was a bit nervous that day. Friends were dropping by to have coffee after lunch. Of course, that meant I had a lot of picking up to do. Then get myself ready. And, of course, the dictator had to be ready to perform too. I was well aware that he was the real reason for the visit—although I suspect that checking on how well (or how poorly) I was handling motherhood was also part of the motive. My head was pounding and it was not even 9:00 A.M. Some of you will say that it is not enough to justify my actions. I know. But wait: I have more excuses.

Because of the headache, I had decided to start with what I thought would create the least amount of protest, and, hence, noise: cleaning up the house. Well, cleaning might be too fancy a word for what is basically hiding most of the mess and clearing the counter. The toddler was getting pretty good at playing by himself for a little while so I figured that I could probably get the dishes cleaned. Well, it turned out he was pretty good every other day. Not this Monday. He clung to me so much that it felt as though I had grown another limb.

I managed to get the house half decent by 11 o'clock, with my third leg in tow. My headache was the size of the Empire State Building when I caught sight of myself in the mirror, blurry image in a spray of window cleaner. Faded leggings and ripped sweatshirt would not do. Hair . . . When was the last time I had a shower? That's when a funny smell hit me, despite the mist of ammonia clouding my head. Either it had been a longer time than I thought since I had seen soap or my extra leg had started to stink.

Getting rid of the smell became the priority. More songs, more games, more vehicles, and he was finally out of his clothes. Another stand-up-comedian routine and he was clean. I debated about leaving him naked until my friends got here in order to save an outfit—baby bellies are so cute! Fearing for my credibility as a suitable mother, though, I opted instead for another one-woman show and managed to get him dressed. But time had flown. It was noon and I had not even brushed my teeth.

Then it hit me. The noise first. Those annoying little voices came on as my son inadvertently pushed the power button on the remote control. Where had that thing been anyway? I had been looking for it for weeks! Then the giggles filled the room. Theirs. And his. That's when the idea made its nasty way into my exhausted mother brain. Just once, I thought, it won't hurt him. Can't scar him for life . . . Can it?

I know I was looking for excuses but you have to understand: I so needed a shower! I closed my eyes and took a deep breath. Excerpts from parenting books started flashing in my head like big neon signs. I opened my eyes. I started hearing parents . . . erm . . . myself, putting down people for . . . erm . . . I shook my head to stop the debate and clenched my teeth. I brought the baby's little chair over, adjusted the volume of the television, kissed the top of his head and watched his eyes start to sparkle. Hey, this was PBS after all. How bad could it be?

Yet I cringed at the sight of the television screen while my son was clearly enthralled by the bright colors, the nonsensical

but strangely hypnotic babbling, and the constant repetition. I
hoped that my friends would not arrive before the end of the
show. And I prayed for forgiveness. I ran into the shower and
enjoyed peace and quiet. And guilt . . . while my son was in
the living room watching what I'd sworn he never would: the
Teletubbies.

• • • • •

Born in la belle province de Québec, **Josée Malo** traded snow-
storms for rain forests and moved to Vancouver Island more
than fifteen years ago to teach sixth-grade French immersion.
She still calls Montreal her home and returns every summer
with her little boy to enjoy the vibrant cultural life.

An Enormous Leap

BY MARNIE SLOANE

I never thought I'd be a parent. Not just because I grew up in the zero-population-growth era, either; I just never felt that urge to create a tenant for my womb.

As the only girl of five, surrounded by two brothers on each side, I think it was supposed to fall to me to be the babysitting/ nurturing one. This was not to be, however, for I found more pleasure in playing rough games with my brothers than creating a rich maternal life for my Barbie. My Barbie loved to make out with Ken and drive her Corvette, but she didn't want to be tied to the stove. No, she and Midge were too busy figuring out how they were gonna meet Paul McCartney and get him to marry me.

Imagine my surprise at thirty when I found myself thinking about what it might be like to have a kid. The dang thought wouldn't go away. It just kept harassing me in tandem with my soon-to-be-husband's mantra-like nightly monologue, "Let's have a baby. Wanna have a baby?"

It was soon after we married that I got pregnant, and truth be told, I never felt better in my life. In fact, if I'd known pregnancy hormones would make me feel that good, I would have done it a lot sooner.

Everybody told me I was gonna have a girl. This fact was based on the generational experience of both sides of the family, not to mention the hordes of relatives I'd inherited through marriage. "She's sitting at the girl angle." "You're carrying the baby low, it's definitely a girl." Everyone who gaped at my amazing belly said the same thing, all except for George, that is. My husband was convinced he had sired a male, and, even though we could have discovered the baby's sex during the ultrasound, I wanted to wait for the surprise.

Turned out George was right, and I gave birth to a healthy baby boy amid lots of screaming on my part due to not choosing an epidural. After the baby came out, someone put a warmed blanket over me and I was in heaven again. Well, for a little while, anyway, since we didn't have a name for this new little creature. George and I fought like the dickens over names for hours before the nurse finally came in and announced the baby had to have a name. I don't know if she was lying to expedite the situation, but we ended up agreeing on Sean, an honorable form of address that was somehow related to George's father's name of John, I said. And so it was.

To say I was unprepared to perform my mothering duties is putting it mildly. I didn't know a baby could come out with fingernails already grown! Luckily my mother stayed with us for three days and showed me some ropes, and I learned little by little, with a lot of mentoring from George plus a few trials and many errors.

Lo and behold our boy grew, and by the time he was four he was a swimming ace who one particular weekend performed a back flip off the rocks at the lake where my adult nephew-in-laws had taken their little cousin swimming. These young men were very responsible and athletic, having become sheriffs and the like, and I trusted that they taught Sean well.

And indeed they did, as I discovered a couple of days later. Knowing nothing about flipping through the air into water, I sat by the pool in our complex watching Sean swim. He was marvelous, holding his breath as he swam underwater the entire length of the short pool, leaping from the diving board like the Olympic divers he'd seen on TV, looking for me every time he emerged from the depths, laughing and saying, "Did you see me, Mommy?"

I went to the edge of the pool and asked, "Hey, baby, do you remember what Phil and Georgie taught you at the lake? Do you remember the flips?" He nodded. I really wanted to see him flip, since I'd been too far away on shore to see him the other day. I asked him if he'd like to show me, and he was a bit hesitant, but wanted to do it. He stood by the edge, toes clamped to the cement, heels dangling over the water. We counted, "Ready? One . . . two . . . three . . . ."

He took an enormous leap, his toddler-sized body moving up and away from the side of the pool. Or so it seemed.

Seconds later, his head clipped the cement edge of the pool, and he bounced rather than slipped into the water.

Time stopped. My heart stopped. Immediately I was filled with disbelief, as if my son hadn't banged his head on the cement and was now facedown in the water. It seemed like it took hours for my body to respond as I watched myself grab first one little arm then the other and pull him from the pool. He looked up at me as I cradled him, a dazed look on his face, while I hated myself with the fiercest loathing of my life. Then he started to cry, and I followed suit, blubbering into his ear, repeating, "I'm sorry, baby, are you okay?"

The doctor reported no concussion, but it was hard to tell what possible damage might come from it, since he still had a toddler skull. I was instructed to watch for blackouts, confusion or pupil dilation among other things, and never to let him back dive into a pool again unless professionally trained and a good sight older. The doctor made it clear that I had made a bad decision, since back dives are not something the average four-year-old should be doing. In fact, he suggested, only prodigy akin to an aquatic Mozart should be permitted to dive, and even then, never off the side of a pool and only with professional supervision. Clearly, not only was I no professional, I was a bad mother who needed supervision herself.

Now sixteen, Sean is a handsome, healthy, extremely practical young man entering his senior year in high school. While I think about that terrifying moment with an eye on what damage I might have allowed to happen, he doesn't seem any worse for wear. And he still loves the water, having turned his love of it toward surfing.

Truth be told, I have no idea how this young man became so responsible and self-assured. You see, I got held back in the school of hard knocks: no common sense. I was too busy thinking about the next party and all the cute boys I was too afraid to approach. When the topic arises, I'm known to say it had nothing to do with me, and, considering just one of the bad decisions I made, I know deep down inside I'm right.

•••••

Sean's mom, **Marnie Sloane,** lived on three continents before the age of ten. Originally from Los Angeles, her family's traveling entourage, including five kids, grandparents, and assorted animals, returned to the States to find life in Southern California full of sun, fun, and irony.

But Momma, I Really Need To Go!

By Rachel Johnson

As a mother of three girls I am rarely alarmed about physical ailments. I know that most of the time, I can nurse my children back to health without taking them to the doctor. The kids do visit the pediatrician regularly for checkups and when they come down with a particularly nasty bug, but I handle most garden-variety kid illnesses (sunburns and sniffles) with ease. There are, however, exceptions.

For about two months my four-year-old, Hayley, asked to go to the potty wherever we were if we were out. We'd be driving down the road and it seemed she would find the most interesting places to declare, "I need to go!" I'd been through this bathroom fascination phase before with my nine-year-old, and I thought Hayley's interest in public restrooms must be starting early. Some of the time I would indulge her, and other times I would insist that she wait until we got home.

"But, I need to go!" was always her response. Of course, I thought she was just playing it up so that she could check out the bathrooms and see if they had a blow dryer or paper towels, automatic flushers or the regular kind. Typical kid sort of thing, I thought. I remember doing it when I was younger.

Then, I noticed that she was going all the time at home, too. It made sense, because she was drinking quite a bit (more in equals more out). But the weather was getting warmer and I figured her increased thirst was because she was spending so much time outside and was fighting dehydration. She didn't have any pain that would indicate a urinary-tract infection, so I figured this too shall pass.

Except her perceived fascination didn't fade, it got worse. I actually started calling her the "girl who couldn't stop peeing" and we would both laugh. Until I realized she really couldn't stop! One night, she got up thirty-two times to go potty! Figuring that she was just trying to keep herself awake, I got upset and told her I didn't want her up again. She cried, and I was angry, but I had more potty time than I could stand!

The next morning Hayley just wasn't right. And she was still going like crazy. This wasn't a joke anymore. I took her to the emergency room to have her checked out. The doctor informed me that the reason for the peeing was that Hayley's blood sugars were over 680 mg/dl. I still didn't get it—until he told me that normal blood sugar levels were between 80 and 120.

My baby has diabetes. My beautiful girl, who had been joking about her all-too-often potty breaks, had an all-too-real reason for all the complaints and pit stops. The thirst had not been a result of the warm spring days, but of the dehydration caused by chronic high blood-sugar levels.

It was a shock, and I felt so guilty for yelling at her the previous night and into the early morning. My baby was really sick, and I didn't even stop to consider it could be more than a fascination with the bathroom until the very end. Even as I was taking her to the hospital, I was thinking it must just be some unusual type of urinary-tract infection.

Insulin brought Haley's blood sugar back under control within hours, and she was quickly back to her old self. Three days later, educated in the art of insulin injections and blood-sugar testing by the medical staff, we left the hospital for home.

I explained my guilt to my daughter, apologized to her for not realizing something was wrong. I was deeply afraid that my anger had scarred her for life.

"It's okay, Momma," she said with ease. "You didn't know that I had diabetes and I would have been mad, too!" She laughed in her easy way and hugged me tight; assuring me in her four-year-old way that there was no permanent damage. Hayley's diabetes has given me new perspective on quite a few things. Formerly minor things like a change in appetite or thirst, fatigue, and of course, a change in bathroom habits now have me running for a blood glucose meter and the doctor's phone number. And while this disease has brought us new challenges to face, it's also brought us closer together.

• • • • •

RACHEL JOHNSON, a freelance writer, currently lives in Texas with her husband, Ryan, and their three beautiful daughters.

Preschool Dropout

BY CHANTAL MEIJER

Our middle child, unlike his siblings, didn't want to go to preschool. And to prove his point, he locked his father out of his truck.

Michael is our third boy, sandwiched between identical twin brothers six years older and his baby sister four years younger. He learned early to be his own man.

The twins had taught me everything I needed to know about raising boys, or so I thought. They had the customary toys—trucks, rocking horses, soccer balls, baseballs and mitts; all the things boys loved to play with and participate in. And, there was the fun-loving, adventure-pleasing preschool. They loved preschool. Like his brothers before him, Michael would love it, too, right?

Michael had his own ideas—about a lot of things. He wasn't the social creature his brothers were. After all, why wouldn't they be social? They always had each other, so they never knew what it was like to play alone. Being six years younger, Michael knew it often. And he didn't always like the same toys as his brothers. Why should he? After observing double toys galore, other toys, unusual ones, piqued his interest. Where his brothers played with Batman and Robin figures, Michael gravitated toward toy wrestlers. Where his brothers loved, even relished, swimming lessons, Michael, who, while still in diapers had sat poolside with his mother watching his brothers swim, decided he had no pressing need to do the same. (He only learned to swim as a teenager by jumping into the pool and instantly swimming across it in a do-or-die maneuver.)

So of course he had his own ideas about preschool: Which would extend to elementary, middle, and high school. But I wanted him to go. That first day, I might as well have been trying to contest gravity.

Being the good mother that I was, I had meticulously checked out all the neighborhood preschools, going so far as to personally observe them in action. At this one school, the kids wore cute uniforms—white shirts, navy sweaters. The staff was impeccable. The toys were to die for. This was the quintessential preschool.

Michael would love it. He'd make new friends. He'd play with new toys. He'd, he'd . . . . He'd hate it! Oh, no! How could he? It was perfect. Okay, even if at first he wasn't delirious at the thought of getting into his cute preschool uniform and skipping off to preschool, he'd come around to it, I reasoned. His brothers had jumped and skipped merrily off to preschool. And because of where we'd lived, their preschool wasn't nearly as nifty as this one.

From the beginning, Michael argued. "I don't want to go," his sweet, but firm four-year-old voice repeated. I had primed him for preschool success, or so I thought, with my gushy "you'll have fun, lots of fun" prep talks. All the little uniform-clad preschoolers seemed gleefully immersed in full fun.

For Michael, full fun meant one thing—and it would take more than myriad false promises of fun at preschool to convince him otherwise—rocking on his chair at home. The large, upholstered living room chair was his oasis. He'd been rocking on it ever since he was a baby. He rocked back and forth, back and forth—before breakfast, after breakfast; before and after lunch; before and after dinner. Occasionally he'd attend to something else, but it had to be more important—like food or wrestlers or a friend calling him outside to play.

And so it came to be that one day, about two weeks after he'd first started, I asked my husband to drop Michael off at preschool. The baby needed attention, or was still sleeping; whatever, I can't really remember, but suffice to say, my motherly hands were tied. Besides, I needed a break from the tug-of-war preschool battle with Michael. He'd have to listen to his dad.

My husband, a Royal Canadian Mounted Police officer, agreed to drop Michael off on his way to work, and so, in full uniform, he scooped up Michael, placed him in the front seat of the SUV, and off they went.

Once at school my husband got out of the vehicle and walked around the front of it to let Michael out. But Michael had had

enough of preschool and this was where he'd make his stand
. . . or, sit, perhaps. He quickly locked all the doors and refused
to get out. His father couldn't get in the car and no amount
of pleading, reasoning, or bribery—and I'm sure my husband
tried them all—could convince Michael to unlock the doors.

I can only imagine—and I did conjure quite the picture as
my husband described the scene to me later—what the two of
them looked like: my husband in full Mountie uniform, con-
versing through the SUV's windows to a I-will-not-budge-four-
year-old. What an incongruous sight—a red-faced Mountie,
with smoke coming out of his ears, pleading with a purse-
lipped, vehicle-commanding four-year-old. Oh, how I wish I'd
been there.

The drama ended when my husband finally convinced
Michael to unlock the doors on the condition that he'd drive
him straight home. "Here's your stubborn kid; he won't go
to school and I give up," he decreed as he unceremoniously
dropped Michael off at our front door. Why is it they're always
"my kids" when he's annoyed and "our" kids when he's not?

I pulled Michael out of preschool. He went back to rocking on his chair. And so the rocking continued—before and
after primary school; before and after high school; and then
after graduation, before and after work. Every time the chair's
rocking mechanism fell apart, which it did frequently over the
years, my husband welded it back together.

Recently Michael, at twenty-one years of age, moved out of
the house and into a place of his own. "His" chair sits in the

living room awaiting transfer to Michael's new house. After my husband attends to another welding job to its undercarriage, the chair will follow its master.

As for his not-so-perfect mother, I imagine my husband and I will still be talking about Michael's short-lived preschool days when we're old and rocking on our own chairs on our front porch.

Fortunately, I'm long past feeling guilty about any of this. It's long been accepted wisdom that a mother who is busy laughing has no time for guilt.

• • • • •

Chantal Meijer lives in Terrace, British Columbia, Canada, with her husband, Rick. They have happily raised four great kids that have all turned out just fine: Mark and Matthew (twins, 27), Michael (21), and Christine (17). Chantal's essays and articles have appeared regionally and nationally in newspapers and magazines.

Marker Mishaps

By Dana Epps

As most parents learn once their child is old enough to crawl, no wall, table, or piece of furniture is safe from the stray pen or marker that gets left within childish grasp. As my mother-in-law discovered on her brand new 800-count Egyptian cotton sheets one afternoon. My eighteen-month-old daughter's budding artistic abilities were taken out upon these sheets in a Jackson Pollock–style slashing. While I felt bad about the sheets, I wouldn't exactly say I felt guilt; it wasn't my fault the sheets were ruined—my mother-in-law had left the permanent marker in my child's reach and it was an inevitable consequence. I was far too savvy to make such an error in my household.

One rainy and boring afternoon, after viewing *Harry Potter and the Chamber of Secrets* for the hundredth time since the video was released, my now three-year-old daughter asked me if she could dress up like Harry Potter. We had the cloak left over from a Halloween costume at our house and we used a stick as a wand. My daughter, always clever and a stickler for doing things the "right way," placed her little hands on her hips and said "but, Mommy, what about my glasses and boo-boo?"

Oh, of course. Harry Potter is hardly Harry Potter without his trademark scar and round glasses. The only problem was that we didn't have a pair of glasses for her to use, and certainly no stick-on scars just lying around. Not being able to stand the disappointed, crestfallen look on my daughter's face, Super Mom, in her attempt to save the day, reaches for the (gasp!) black marker my daughter has been forbidden to use anywhere except in her coloring books.

The giggles and look of complete awe and excitement on her face filled me with joy and pride at my quick, cool-mom thinking. I had drawn on my sweet little child's face a pair of perfectly round spectacles and a lightning-shaped scar. She was thrilled!

It was only until the end of the day after many pretend spells had been cast and the villain was defeated that I attempted to scrub the glasses and scar off her face. I then discovered the marker I used was not only *not* meant to be used on skin, as it was not the washable Crayola brand, it stubbornly refused to be removed at all!

For a full week my daughter went to preschool, the market and church with a faded pair of black spectacles and a faint lightning-shaped scar tattooed on her face. Suffice it to say, since then my daughter and husband give me the finger shake and the "no-no's" when they see me reach for a marker. My daughter admonishingly tells me "Mommy, we draw on the paper, not on the face!"

After the many "no-no's" and countless lectures about the proper use of markers and crayons, I have to admit I feel a bit guilty about hypocritically breaking the rule myself. So, maybe a perfect mom would know better than to use permanent marker on her child's face, but I think my daughter had a lot more fun with her less-than-perfect mom that day.

• • • • •

Dana Epps is the mother of a lively preschooler. Many of her trial-and-error child-rearing stories stem from her lack of sleep as she struggles to balance a career in counseling, a master's degree in psychology, motherhood, wifedom . . . and her own needs, too. She loves every challenging minute of it!

Special

BY SARAH EDDENDEN

Sara likes preschool. When I ask her what she did today, she always answers, "Everything."

She looks particularly cute, two messy ponytails sprouting from each side of her head, each wrapped at the end with a bright pink elastic, light pink flower barrettes trying desperately to hold back stray hairs. She wears a bright yellow top with flower decals on it and the scripted word "girl" along the bottom, blue runners, and green capris.

She swings her Dora doll around and around and giggles, as we wait in the anteroom for the doors to open.

There are other parents, mostly moms, and their children.

Sara smiles at them and says hello too loudly, then, when they don't answer her, says hello again.

The girl in the zebra-striped tights and purple Calvin Klein dress, approaches Sara with a smug smile. I watch.

This little girl is usually aloof. If there are assigned roles to a preschool class, I would name her the "One Who Thinks She Is Better Than the Others." Her mother wears fur-lined sweaters and big diamond rings, has never met my eye or said hello, and calls her child "beautiful," rather than by her actual name.

Sara smiles at Kennedy.

"I have a Dora doll," Sara tells her.

"I'm having a birthday party," Kennedy says in turn, "and I'm not going to invite you."

I'm not sure, from this point on, if my world goes purple and frantic and queasy and blurred on its own, or if it follows Sara's lead. I think, the former. I've had forty years of experience at this. She's just starting out. I do think, by the look on her face, that she thinks, "I'm not sure what to do with that."

Beyond that, I think she thinks, "When I get into the classroom, I'm going to play with the castle first."

I, on the other hand, am already on the floor, knees digging into Kennedy's chest, hands pulling at two neat little braids, telling her she's a rude little girl and who wants to go to her stupid party, anyway?

Not really.

Her mother is off to one side, talking to another mom. When Kennedy walks away from Sara, I see her mom look over and say to her, "Do you want an invitation for Adelaide?"

And Kennedy says, "No."

So her mother goes back to talking with the other mom.

Sara makes her way to my side and tells me what Kennedy said. I run a hand over her messy blond hair and tell her . . .

Actually, I say nothing for a moment. I think I've swallowed my tongue. I'm in pain. I want to cry. I want to yell at Kennedy's

• •

mom—who is now handing an invitation to another young girl that I guess Kennedy has approved—that her daughter is mean and needs to be told what she is doing is wrong. I want to wrap Sara under my arm and take her away, back home, and tuck her where it will be warm and quiet and nice forever.

So finally, I say, "What Kennedy did was not very nice."

I think some more. Sara plays with a string hanging from my sweater. Then I add, "You are a very special girl."

The classroom door opens and Sara runs off, yelling how she wants the castle first. I walk in and drop her reading book off in the drop-off box, wave at the teacher, wave at Sara and leave. And I wait outside for Kennedy's mom and I . . .

Give her the evil eye? The frowning of a lifetime? A big fat, painful titty twister?

I go home.

When I come back to pick Sara up, I am more together. I've had a cry, I've made myself some tea, and I've called my husband.

"Who wants to go to her party if that's the way she acts?" he says to me, and this rings so true, most of the hurt slips away.

I'm just left with a feeling of sadness. Somewhere along the way, someone has let Kennedy believe that it is okay to behave this way. Worse still, that it is fun to behave this way.

I want to say something to her mother, I tell my husband.

"Don't," he says. "She won't give a damn what you have to say."

And he's right, again.

Sara is happy to see me. She races over and hugs my legs and shows me the necklace she made. We walk out to the car, and I get her in her car seat and she sings a new song.

I pull out of the parking lot, and I say, "You know what Kennedy said to you before?"

I see her nod in my rearview mirror.

"I don't ever want you to say that to anybody. You understand?"

She nods.

"Mom?"

"Yes?"

"Can I invite Kennedy to my birthday party?"

I smile. She is something else. She is my wonderful, happy, unexclusionary little girl.

"No," I tell her.

• • • • •

SARAH EDDENDEN's work has been produced on stage and radio in Toronto. She's been published in *Suite 101*'s short story anthology and numerous webzines, including *Tattoo Highway, Zone Mom,* and *Outsider Ink,* where she is currently assistant fiction editor. She is a regular contributor to *http://thewriting bug.com,* and *http://littlebytesnews.com.*

Teaching Meloni to Play

BY MARY V. GROVEMAN

When my daughter, Meloni, started the second grade, I was called for a visit with her teacher. It seemed that Mrs. White was concerned for Meloni because she had trouble socializing with the kids in her class. I was told that when asked why she didn't want to be their friend, my perfect little girl (she really was perfect then) informed the teacher that the other children were babies and she didn't play with babies. Well, I had always known that Meloni was somewhat more mature and possibly brighter than most kids her age, but I didn't see it as a problem.

Mrs. White suggested that I teach Mel how to play like a seven-year-old. I had to let her know that it was okay to get dirty and scream like a banshee once in a while. Meloni needed to be a kid and it was up to me to teach her.

The next afternoon when Meloni got off the school bus, I had surprises waiting for her. First was a snack of chocolate cake and Kool-Aid. I figured the rest would be more enjoyable if she experienced a sugar rush. Next I introduced her to the

• •

pleasure of walking barefoot in the mud. I had let the garden hose run wild in the backyard and the mud puddle I created would have serviced twenty hogs.

It took quite a bit of cajoling on my part to get Meloni to even consider the mud puddle as a source of entertainment, but she finally stepped in.

Okay, so where did I go wrong? Well, I was never a prissy little girl. I was a tomboy through and through. Mud and sugar were my friends, soap and shoes the enemies. So since I was trying to teach my daughter to play, I thought . . . well, yes, I pushed her in the mud. And as my baby girl looked up at me with her muddy, tear-streaked face, I felt my heart break.

Needless to say, I paid hell trying to make up for my bad judgment. As for her acting more like a child, she's nineteen now, doesn't want to leave home, has a collection of stuffed animals worthy of a Guinness record and still calls me Mommy. Meloni has also promised me that when, not if, she starts therapy, she will be sure to bring this up in session—along with everything else.

• • • • •

Mary V. Groveman is a married mother of two amazing kids. She has lived across the United States and South Korea but currently resides in Missouri. She says her life is a jumble of ups and downs, feasts and famines, tears of sadness and joy— it's life in general.

Letting Them Lead

By Juli Hiatt Caldwell

I always thought I would be the quintessential nature mom. My lovely children and I would spend hours wandering around, reveling in nature's majesty. Our food would be nutritious and organic fare, some of which we grew in our own garden. I would give birth completely naturally and medicine-free, maybe squatting over a small ditch in a hut Zuni style. I would lead my daughters through a world of joy, imparting my wisdom, bonding with them through loving educational guidance. I would do this mothering thing on my own terms.

Yeah, right.

Only a woman expecting her first child really thinks these sorts of irrational thoughts. All of my goals were noble ones, but just beyond the realm of what was likely for me at the time. As a new mother recovering from an emergency C-section, I was lucky to accomplish getting my teeth brushed and putting on real clothes after my first daughter came around.

Still, as we became used to each other and I grew into myself as a mother, I set goals for us. My highest priority as a parent was that I would raise a smart child, not a spawn of mindless pop culture. So the TV goes into lockdown and our days are filled with trips to the library and the park, mommy-and-me classes, and other media-free adventures. But as she prepares to enter kindergarten, I find myself filled with trepidation. How will she relate when her friends want to play Power Puff girls?

When my second daughter came along, due to uterine scarring, I would have to give birth once again via C-section. No squatting in the mud the second time around either. Once again, I had to find the compromise between what I wanted and what was possible. I would be sawed in half yet again, and this baby would have to be my last. Rule number one for parents: expect now that what you want and what actually happens may never be the same thing.

With two, I am completely outnumbered. So is my organic optimism. My rules have whittled down from many rules and sub-rules, complete with instruction guide and user's manual, to just a few basic guidelines: don't watch too much TV (I do keep it to PBS Kids and educational DVDs); keep the art projects off my walls and floors (using each other is fine as long as you bathe afterward without flooding the bathroom); don't kill yourselves doing dangerous stunts; and don't kill each other if at all possible. Any cleaning up you do is greatly appreciated, but I'm not holding my breath! Please eat something nutritious in the course of the day, and in case you're wondering, peanut butter is included on my list . . . and I don't mean all-natural organic peanut butter either.

I am starting to wonder if somehow my second daughter has gotten shortchanged. She seems incapable of doing little things that I took for granted with my first. My oldest, for example, knew all her colors, shapes, animals, and their sounds by the time she was two. If I show my youngest a picture of a cow, she says, "Moo!" If I show her a picture of a monkey, she says, "Moo." If I show her a picture of a sheep, she will pause, look at me for some prompting, and say, "Moo?" All letters are "A, B, Z is for Zebra!" Don't get me started on her math skills.

When I had my first, I had dreams and goals that I pushed onto my daughter. I never realized until she started preschool that she was there because I wanted her there. I wanted to build her social skills, but the preschool I selected was a horrible fit for her personality and learning abilities. She was much more content and much better adjusted when I pulled her out and we used workbooks at home, supplementing play dates twice a week to build her social skills. To her credit, she is smarter and doing much better than she should when I consider how many ridiculous activities I pushed on her.

This is why, above all, I will not force my second daughter into anything she does not want. So what if she thinks all animals say moo? At two, this is adorable. If she still thinks this at five, then I will start to worry. So what if she hasn't accomplished everything her sister had by that age? She is a completely different individual, and when her sister goes to kindergarten, she and I will play catch-up together. I will be able to give her the time I gave her sister before she was born, and I'll let her lead with her natural interests, abilities, and talents as they manifest themselves. For now, I will sit back contentedly as she and her older sister and best friend crawl around on the floor, oblivious that I am watching just a few feet away, meowing at each other as their vivid imaginations carry them through a game of cats or lions or house, or whatever they think will be fun, right then at that moment. This is what childhood is all about, and I'm going to let them live it on their terms . . . as long as they don't kill each other doing it.

• • • • •

Juli Hiatt Caldwell is coauthor of the novel *Beyond Perfection*. She lives in Florida, where she spends her days as her children's chauffeur volunteering at the school, writing, and trying to clean the cat hair off her couch.

Television Terminator

By Jorja Jones

My son is not a social pariah.

He has survived twenty-six years, and is heading his own successful design agency. He is five years married—no children yet, though he assures me they will come—and plays tennis and basketball. An accomplished musician, he occasionally lets me come to one of his "gigs" at the hip local pizza joint. A well-rounded individual, he even still goes to church most Sundays.

With all of this in mind I breathe a sigh of relief. It wasn't always like this, and I often feared that I might have ruined him with a pseudo spur-of-the-moment decision made in his early teens.

The week after his thirteenth birthday, in fact, was when it all came to pass. A wet week in late October. He had been particularly obnoxious after coming home from some "stoopid" school outing, and my temper was fraying badly. He was maturing much too quickly for my liking, and I couldn't remember the last time we'd had a great time together.

This rainy evening saw dinner on the table, but mysteriously, no diners. Animated Ninja Turtles were far more captivating, and the husband was of course much too absorbed in the paper to be any help. I don't remember exactly what blew my Vesuvius; there are vague memories of a bad haircut and stubborn postal clerks. But when I came to, I was stomping down the basement stairs with the TV in my arms, power and aerial cables flailing wildly behind me. Padlock firmly in place on the cupboard door, wailing teen at the table, I distinctly remember a warm inner satisfaction at the disbelief plastered on the faces of both the males of my house.

And so I embarked on one of the most determined journeys of my life.

At first, it was smooth sailing. My son didn't revolt, as I feared he might. He was penitent and eager to please, after coming to terms with the shock. I believe that his father may have had an earnest word with him sometime soon after the meal was over—the boob tube was dear to both of them. But I wouldn't cave too soon, this was punishment, and I am not an easy mark. The head man of the house found his own solution when I pointed out that the local bar provided most everything that he watched, on a megalithic screen and with pint-wielding waitresses on hand. His subordinate had no such alternative.

At about day three he must have realized that this was not a fad—the padlock was as stern as my expression, and our tool shed was newly and inexplicably locked. He tried the silent treatment for a day, but that was my forte, and he knew it. Next

came the arguments. He plied me with rationale after rationale. He questioned my sanity. He tried to pull our alpha male
into it, but my husband knows when to stand down.

His trump card was the guilt trip. "Don't you think this is
a bit harsh?" "I've learned my lesson!" and "All my friends get
to watch TV," he said as frequent refrains. But "How long must
this last?!" was the question that made me stop and think.

For months before the confiscation I had been pondering
what nagged me about our family. We used to be a fully func-
tional and thriving unit. But something was missing in recent
times, and I wanted to bring us back together. Was it the blar-
ing box in the living room? I know that it couldn't be the sole
perpetrator, but whenever I walked in on my men, I found it
hard to bear the vacant stares. In truth, I had contemplated
quietly pawning the television while they were both out, but
could never bring myself to face the consequences. I knew that
punishment was incidental: I had merely seized an opportunity to do what I'd dreamed about for months. This is what I
wanted, and I knew that it had to be for the long haul to heal
our family. But did I have the stamina?

After two, maybe three weeks I stopped hearing about the
tragedy of the TV. It might have had something to do with the
trip to Club Med Bali that I extracted from my loving partner.
Or the new allowance that junior was given. Regardless, my
decision to "See how we do without it" was taken on board with
a grunt and sighs worthy of any B-list actor. Sure, I inwardly
cringed when he had friends around and the talk turned to

the latest show. It pained me to see him left out of the *Knight Rider* and *A-Team* discussion with classmates.

But instead of shoe kicking and sofa slumping, I got a boy in my kitchen after school snacking on leftovers and making conversation. There was a healthier sheen, an active mind, a loss of weight. Gone was the mindless couch crashing after dinner, and we made more time for us as a family. Previously ignored delights like fresh air and the outside became firm friends, and the benefit was obvious as the weeks turning to months turned to years.

My son now owns a television, a great widescreen whopper. He has his old parents over to watch a game every now and then, and grins at me when I shake my head. "I still love you, Mom," he whispers, then almost crushes me in a bear hug before slouching next to his father who, it must be said, gets more joy out of the silver siren than the rest of us put together.

I make no claim that television is of the devil, but I know that the happiness I got from its demise was heaven sent.

● ● ● ● ●

Jorja Jones is mother to one, wife to another, and (apparently) personal assistant to both. When she isn't looking after or writing about her men, Jorja keeps herself busy working in public health care. The Joneses play at being a happy family in Vancouver, Canada.

Science Experiment

By Karen Carlucci

After seventeen years as a research scientist I decided that it was time for me to stay home with my four children. I often do little demonstrations and experiments with my children in an attempt to foster an interest in the science field. Most experiments go as planned.

When my oldest daughter was four I bought her a tadpole kit. The kit contained everything needed for tadpoles to grow into frogs; all we had to do was order the tadpoles. I thought this would be a great demonstration for my daughter. I quickly ordered the tadpoles. When they arrived we placed them in water, added their food, and watched them grow. It wasn't long before the tadpoles grew into frogs. My daughter was very excited about the success of this biological demonstration.

The frogs needed more upkeep than the butterflies we grew the previous year and set free within three weeks. The water had to be changed frequently or the frogs would smell. The fresh water had to be very hot and then allowed to cool before the frogs were placed in the container. This procedure eventually began to become burdensome, and I wondered silently about the lifespan of frogs, but my daughter enjoyed watching me each time as I dutifully cleaned the container.

One day while I was cleaning the frogs' container I got distracted and forgot to let the water cool. As my daughter watched, I dumped the frogs back into the container of hot water and immediately gasped as their little bodies convulsed for about five seconds and then went completely still. Horrified, I quickly turned to my daughter.

I searched her little face for a reaction, wondering how I was ever going to comfort her and get her through such a traumatic experience. She looked at me with big round eyes, blinked several times, then furrowed her brow and calmly said, "Some scientist you are." I stayed in the kitchen with the dead frogs for more than an hour, crying my eyes out. But my daughter was completely unruffled. She turned around, walked into the family room, and began to watch one of her favorite cartoons.

I'm happy to report that that little frog experiment six years ago didn't dampen my daughter's interest in science. In fact, she says she wants to be a zoologist when she grows up. I hope she does better at frog experiments than her mom did.

• • • • •

Karen Carlucci spent many years as a research scientist seeking new ways to fight diseases. She now spends her days seeking new ways to find sanity as a stay-at-home mom with four children. Being a writer helps.

My Secret Weapon

By Michelle Capasso

As a soon-to-be mother of three under three, I'm used to the unusual looks and remarks I get from total strangers. While out with my two rambunctious toddlers, I find people feel compelled to judge my very pregnant state. Comments range from the subtle "I don't envy you" to the oh-so-polite "Did you mean for this to happen?" But the one question that virtually everyone asks is how I manage to get anything done, assuming my life is total chaos.

At that point, I usually give my stock answer: "It's tough in the beginning, but then everybody falls into a routine, and it's actually fairly calm." As for the truth? Well, I can get a lot done, and things are fairly calm most of the time, due to my secret weapon: lots and lots of TV.

Not that I would ever admit that to anyone. What kind of mother would want to own up to the fact that the television set is on way over the American Academy of Pediatrics' recommended limit of two hours a day? In our house, it's more like twelve hours a day, to be exact. And that is just for the kids programming, never mind the nighttime programming that my husband and I watch during our "alone" time.

But during play groups and music class, I'll nod and agree with all the other mothers, talking about how we only play music for our kids during the day, that we help them color or play with their toys. After story circle at the library, I'll pretend we already picked out our books while my kids jump all over the video rental rack.

What I want to know is how can anyone keep a household running without help from a steady stream of entertainment? Do they actually entertain their kids themselves?

Of course, I tell myself that this is okay, that my kids are actually learning things from the shows and videos that they watch incessantly. I turn a deaf ear to the constant media warnings of lower IQ scores, future attention-deficit disorders and aggressive behavior due to heavy TV watching. Instead, I comfort myself in noting that my daughter knew her alphabet and could count to twenty by eighteen months old, courtesy of *Sesame Street*. I remind myself that my son can identify classical music tunes by their composer; thanks to the never-ending stream of Baby Einstein DVDs (we own twelve of them). And it's not like they just sit there, catatonic—they sing, dance, and play to whatever selection happens to be on at the time. It's just tough to explain at play dates why my child is begging for the TV to be on while in a room full of new and exciting toys.

And it's not like I let them watch just anything that comes on television. I stick to channels that are "noncommercial."

. . . .

Although I realize the noncommercial status is pretty much a joke—that fifteen-second sponsor tag on PBS is all my child needs to memorize the tag line and jingle from McDonald's or to recognize the colors of the Dunkin' Donuts logo before he could read. That's a tough one to explain away in play group. As is my son's constant conversational references to Baby Einstein or "Baby Giraffe" or "Sea Turtles"—he recognizes the DVDs by the pictures imprinted on their surfaces.

The part about the "routine" that keeps the chaos to a minimum is entirely true. I don't mention that our routine is built around the programming schedule of our favorite channels— breakfast to *Sesame Street*, playtime until *Reading Rainbow*, into naps before the end of *Mr. Rogers' Neighborhood* reruns, and dinner by the time of *Zoom*'s second airing of the late afternoon. It's almost like a giant clock, keeping me on schedule throughout the day.

And while they are entertained and educated, I keep my sanity by getting things done—laundry, cleaning, cooking, etc. I'll take a quick run down to check e-mail while a favorite video is running; maybe check into some chatrooms while I am at it. I can't be the only one doing this, can I? At least someone else must laugh during the opening of the *Baby Einstein* series, showing the mother sitting on the floor, "interacting" with her child while the video is playing. I throw the DVD in and run, trying to seize as much time for myself as possible while the video captures their attention. Half the time, I'm not entirely sure what's actually on these videos—I just trust the brand name. When my friend mentioned how painful it is to watch The Wiggles' *Spaghetti Western*, I just nodded along silently in agreement—I had never actually watched the thing myself.

But is it really so bad? My kids are actually less aggressive than their peers and are right on track when it comes to learning and development. They are not hyperactive and actually are very good and well-behaved, as toddlers go. Could all the dire warnings of TV watching be hyped-up news bites aimed to make already stressed parents feel even guiltier? I was one of the first generations to grow up with *Sesame Street,* and I consider myself well-educated and responsible. Then again, I did work in television for thirteen years, so maybe I'm also biased.

Unfortunately, as my kids grow into preschoolers, the TV is no longer the panacea that it once was. It simply does not hold their attention as long as it used to, and while I still run off and handle some chore after popping in a video, I'll now find them getting into some kind of trouble, instead of sitting there in a mesmerized state. Apparently the new *Baby Neptune* DVD wasn't as much fun as mashing an entire tube of Desitin ointment into my leather couches while I visited a writers' chatroom. And while I assume he's enjoying *Blue's Clues*, my oldest is getting pretty handy at sneaking out of the house and waving to the neighbors from our deck in his underwear. (Thankfully, we are new in the neighborhood so no one knows us well enough to call DSS.)

I'm saddened at the loss of my "electronic babysitter." I'm finding that it's a lot harder to get things done when I actually have to watch my kids most of the day. My husband doesn't know about all the TV (although I guess the secret will be out when he reads this book), but he definitely notices the decline in productivity around here. But at least I can hold out hope that this next baby will find the TV as enchanting as my older two.

•••••

Michelle Capasso is a writer and mom living in Westchester County, New York. The odds are good that her three children, including the newborn, are watching television at this very moment.

A Question of Commitment

By Sonia Beaumont

I was eighteen and determined not to end up a soccer mom. I was twenty with a newborn girl and could guarantee I would be the fabulous mom to have the great job in the fashion industry and still be around to help with the homework.

Now I am thirty and taking a good look back at the mom I have finally become.

My girlfriends and I discuss how this has happened. And there are many moments when, staying up late cutting and pasting Valentines together, I ask myself too. And there are even more moments when the kids are screaming at each other that I ask my husband how this all came to be. To me, it seems unreal. This cannot possibly be my life. Not for me—I was going to have an awesome career in the fashion world. With no kids at all.

When I was young I loved the whole fashion scene. Normal children were playing dodge ball and red rover and I would sit out every gym class and recess for fear of ruining my freshly purchased clothes. My parents didn't know what to do with me.

They didn't even know what a Fendi or Gucci was. While I was a teenager I modeled and it only fueled my fire. I entered college determined to be a fashion buyer. I hooked myself up with a terrific internship at a buying office and was on my way.

God had other plans.

Marisa was born when I was twenty and unmarried. I took a semester off and then headed back to college. She was four by the time I graduated and part of what made that moment so special was seeing her face in the crowd as I walked across the stage. I continued with my plans for my career, still working in the buying office. My foot was in the door. By now I was married to a wonderful man who supported my plans and dreams. And we both wanted a baby. Giovanni was born when I was twenty-four.

After this pregnancy I knew some things would have to change. I took a longer maternity leave and asked to return part-time to my job. My company agreed, but it was probably the kiss of death. I did love my job, I still enjoyed being part of the fashion industry but somehow it just didn't all fit together in a nice little package anymore. Trying to find a balance, trying to get over the guilt of being a working mom definitely took its toll. But I told myself that this was what I had always wanted to do, and I had worked so hard, I had to go for it. This was my dream! So a promotion came up within the company and I applied. I didn't get the job. So I asked my boss for some constructive criticism. She was very evasive. I went to Human Resources for some answers. Here was their response, "You didn't receive the promotion because we question your commitment to your family."

That stupid little sentence changed my life. I knew that deep down I had become a full-fledged mom. As much as I tried to fight it, those little faces won. It felt like I was letting go of so much baggage to admit it myself. I no longer cared that I never owned a Louis Vuitton purse or that I wouldn't be chatting with New York showrooms everyday. I worked hard for that company and I was as talented as anyone there. I wasn't willing to work ten-hour days to "prove" how committed I was to the company. Or to prove how uncommitted I was to my family. I knew I might have some regrets over my next move, but nothing in my life would ever be more important than my family.

I didn't get angry. I didn't cry. I told Human Resources, "I guess I need to question my commitment to your company." I handed in my two-week notice that afternoon.

That was four years ago. And there have been some regrets. It is tough to hear about some of my college classmates' awesome jobs and their monthly travels to New York. I hear a voice in my head, saying, "It's supposed to be me! That was supposed to be my job!" And on a daily basis I become frustrated with my life. But there are lots of different careers out there for me. I know something will fit into my life the way I need it to. There are many mothers out there that feel completely fulfilled by motherhood. That isn't me. Yet, I still don't know how to balance the career and the family. But I will find a career that understands the priorities and responsibilities I have as a woman and a mother.

I try not to think of all the things I wish I had done or could do. Instead I think of all the things I do have. How Marisa and Giovanni make me feel a love deeper than I ever knew existed. How they make me appreciate and understand my own parents in a whole new way. How they have made me dissect my own thoughts and feelings. How I can look at them each day and see firsthand the miracle of life.

Now, I am almost thankful for my career's (temporary) demise. I feel like saying: "Thank you Company X for making me realize it's not about what I will never have, but about all the blessings that were sitting right in my lap."

So I am not a soccer mom. But I was the Girl Scout leader. I am no longer a model. But my daughter's friends all tell me that they wish their moms dressed cool like me. I will never be a fashion buyer. But it's okay. God gave me something more. So much more that I didn't even know I wanted it. He made me a mother. And of all the things I will accomplish in my life, this job is definitely number one.

• • • • •

Sonia Beaumont currently lives in New Berlin, Wisconsin, with her husband, Robert, and two children, Marisa (11) and Giovanni (6). Her family has shaped her life in a way that she never knew was possible and also has strengthened her faith and relationship with God.

Damned If You Do

BY MARCIA J. WILSON

I think that single moms have a hard time of it. I was a single mom for ten years and during that time I raised four children with the added bonus of a surprise grandchild. I worked full-time to support my brood and went to school full-time in the hopes of improving our circumstances.

Talk about guilt. I woke up early, commuted an hour to work, got home late, or went straight to school, and basically was never home except during sleeping hours and on weekends. During that time period my children suffered. Talk about guilt.

No. Really it's all about choice. I had to make choices. I wasn't lucky enough to receive child support or alimony. So I had to decide whether to avail myself of the aid available to women with children, more fondly known as welfare, or to work my proverbial buns off trying to make ends meet. Either way, a lot of guilt was involved. At the time it looked like a lose-lose situation. Stay home with the kids and feel guilty about being on welfare, or not be at home with the kids and feel guilty about not being home.

I am not critical of the single-mother friends I had who elected to use the aid available to them. I was jealous in a way. I am not critical of the working moms. I was a working mom who wanted to be home for my children, but couldn't be. I tried to think of the "higher path," that of setting an example of hard work and education for my children. Meanwhile, all they wanted was some of my time, a shoulder to cry on, some advice, baked cookies, and maybe a cuddle now and then. I was so darn tired every night that I literally fell into an exhausted sleep as soon as I lay down.

My children took turns getting into serious trouble while being left unattended. I had them in a home day care after school until the oldest was fifteen years old and could watch over them, at which time she decided she didn't want that responsibility and went into a full-blown rebellion. That's how my first grandson came into being. The second daughter decided that she didn't want to live at home and tried living with her father, then her grandmother and finally at eighteen years old, she bolted. The third child, the one and only son, got into trouble at school, got into drugs, and struggled with bouts of depression. The fourth daughter was happily in her own little world, however she got into the habit of sneaking food into her room, watching TV, and eating until she turned into a very large little girl.

Those years were harder than anything I can remember. Was I a good mom? I don't know. I know I tried. I got up early every Saturday morning and cleaned the house, did the laundry, yard work, and grocery shopping . . . often all completed by noon. As my children arose from their slumber I cooked them a big breakfast and tried to spend time with each one of them, listening to their stories about their lives. I took them to church on Sunday mornings and tried to interact with them during the day, making sure that their homework was completed, knew what their chores for the week were, and that I knew what was going on with each of them. I tried to take them individually along when I had to run errands, so that I could give each of them some "mommy time." But, it wasn't enough. It just wasn't enough.

I know that kids get into trouble and do bad things even when they have an intact family with both well-adjusted parents in the home. But this was not what I had dreamed about when I wanted to start a family. I could not even try to be the perfect mom. The deck was stacked against me, against us.

It was a hard road. But I have to tell you that now that they are young adults, each and every one of them is well-adjusted, self-supporting, educated, or getting educated. We are all very close and talk on the phone and by e-mail every single day. I feel that they love me and appreciate me. I have asked them each to forgive me for any failings of mine that they felt. We've talked about what happened and how it happened. It seems that now they understand why I chose the path and why they suffered for it. Many times they have told me, individually, that they are very proud of their mother and believe that they can do anything because "Mom did it."

What is interesting to me is that I still feel the guilt. I can see with my own eyes that the kids and I made it through the toughest of times together. I know in my heart that each of them is on solid ground now. My mother calls the guilt I feel, "false guilt." The truth is that I did my best, like mothers do. We make choices in life and we have no guarantee of the outcome. We can keep a vision in our heads of the right way to live, take the "higher road," and all we can do is do what we think is right in each moment of every day, and pray for the best.

• • • • •

Marcia J. Wilson is the mother of six children and two grandchildren. When her children were small, she experienced a devastating divorce and was a single mom for ten years. While raising her children she completed a master's degree and specialized in information-technology security as a profession.

Mom's Little Helper

By Darleen Principe

I had my son Francis at the age of seventeen, only two days before my high school graduation. Now I'm trying to secure our future by graduating from college and finding a steady career.

I go to school in the mornings, work in the afternoons, and spend my evenings with my son. He goes to school in the mornings as well, and then he stays at a day care until after I get off work. We live at home with my parents and my two younger brothers, and as the baby of the house he gets more than his share of love and attention.

I consider Francis to be a very clever and caring kid. Although I regret not being able to spend every waking moment with him, he seems to understand our situation. He tries to help out as much as he can, and most of the time he's actually quite the mommy's little helper.

One evening when Francis was four, I picked him up from day care. We came home and he immediately went to the television. I sat down with him and because I had had a long day,

I accidentally fell asleep. Maybe half an hour later, I woke up and he was nowhere to be seen.

The first thing I did was go upstairs to see if he was in the bedroom playing with his toys. As I reached the top stair, I noticed a trail of white powder scattered across the hall and into the bedroom. I walked into the room and there he was, pouring baby powder all over the carpet.

I walked toward him, took away the baby powder, told him that he had done a bad thing and made him sit in the corner with a time-out. He began to cry. I remained firm, and told him that he had to stay in that corner until I cleaned up the mess, and then we would have to talk about what he'd done.

I vacuumed up the baby powder as best as I could, and then went over to him and began to scold him. He just sat in that corner and listened to me tell him that what he did was wrong, little tears running down his face. Finally, I asked him, "Why did you do that?"

"You were tired and I was surprising you," he said.

I snapped back at him, "That was not a very nice thing to do! What were you thinking?"

His answer was, "The white stuff makes the carpet smell good."

My attitude changed, immediately. I picked him up out of the corner and smothered him with hugs and kisses, apologizing. I finally put him down and the first thing he said after that was, "Are you mad at me, Mom?" I must have confused him with my sudden change in attitude.

I had recognized right away the logic behind the baby powder. That past weekend, I had spread powder carpet freshener before vacuuming the carpet. He was watching me while I was vacuuming and expressed his excitement about how nice the carpet smelled because of the "white stuff."

He was only trying to help me clean. He intended to spread "white stuff" all over the carpet, then to vacuum it up so when I woke up from my nap, I would be so proud of him for doing it. Instead, I woke up, got angry, and gave him a time-out.

I felt like such a horrible mother for assuming the worst before I'd even asked him for an explanation. Would my initial reaction to his kind gesture scar him for life? I hoped I hadn't discouraged him from doing anything nice for me ever again.

I sat down next to him and explained that I hadn't known he was trying to do something nice and that I was so sorry for yelling at him, and that I was definitely not mad at him.

I did end up explaining that baby powder was the wrong "white stuff" to use on the carpet, and that next time he should wait for me if he wanted to clean it up. I told him I would give him the right powder to use and that I would help him vacuum.

I asked him what I could do to make it up to him. He said he wanted to go buy a new toy. Under normal circumstances, I probably wouldn't have just gone out and bought him a new toy, but I felt so bad for misjudging him that I couldn't say no. I took him out with me and ended up buying him a new action figure. I was so relieved to see a smile on his face again.

It's been almost two years since that little incident, and I'm still not sure if I fully recovered from my horrible reaction. I still feel a little guilty, but if it taught me anything, it taught me to think of what he could be trying to do before I jump to any bad conclusions.

Now that Francis is six years old, he's still very keen on helping me out with anything I'm doing. I'm a little more confident now that I didn't scar him for life, and my only conclusion is that my son is very observant and clever for trying to do what he did. And I'm proud that he has the biggest heart I've ever known.

● ● ● ● ●

Darleen Principe is currently a student at California State University Northridge, pursuing a bachelor's degree in magazine journalism. She is working as a scriptwriter for a communications marketing company and hopes to extend her skills in mass print media. Darleen is a single mother of one child, Francis, and hopes to one day expand her family.

Lost in Toddler Translation

By Cynthia Potts

As a mother of two young daughters, I'm rapidly learning that it doesn't matter exactly what you say to your children. It's how they interpret your words that matters.

For example, I had enlisted then three-year-old Harmony in some pretty intensive housecleaning. She'd been pitching in like a trooper, wielding the Dustbuster with almost professional skill and emptying can after can of Pledge on our coffee table.

Then we got to the bathroom. I had her "scrub the tub" while I was attending to the toilet. Her interest in her assigned task quickly paled, especially while mommy was using some neat stuff in a spray can that made big, huge bubbles.

"No, Harmony, stay away," I told her. "This is a Mr. Yuck." She backed off half a step, but I could see she was still intrigued. So I kept explaining, "Besides which, this is a *stinky* potty!"

Harmony was entranced. "We have a stinky potty! We have a stinky potty!" She sang this delightful lyric the entire time we worked in the bathroom. Then we moved on to another room, and I thought no more about it.

• •

Later, I was relaxing with a cup of coffee when suddenly I realized it was quiet. Too quiet.

"Harmony, what are you doing?" I called.

She ran into the room, beaming a triumphant smile. "I did it, Mommy! I fixed the potty!" Chubby arms waved in the air. "Come see!"

"What do you mean you fixed the potty?" I asked, rapidly following her down the hall.

"It's not stinky anymore!" she announced, throwing open the bathroom door. "I fixed it."

And there, floating in the bowl, were at least six bottles of my perfume! Harmony had emptied the entire contents of my vanity into the toilet. The air was filled with the mingled scents of jasmine, vanilla, and Tidy Bowl.

Even better, kids remember what you say to them, no matter how offhand and trivial the comment might be.

I'm a freelance writer. My career was getting off the ground when Harmony started kindergarten. She knew I was eager to find writing work, so she was puzzled to hear me declining a job offer from a lady we'd met in the grocery store.

"Why don't you want to write for that lady, Mommy?"

"Because she wanted me to put together a sixteen-page newsletter twice a month for her group for free, honey. We don't write for free in this family." My quick-and-simple answer seemed to satisfy her, and I didn't have to get into a long, detailed explanation of hobby vs. career, or art vs. commerce, for which I was very thankful.

• •

The conversation was forgotten, until a few days later when Harmony came home from kindergarten, furious.

"What's the matter?"

She dug into the depths of her Spiderman book bag, retrieving a homemade book. Construction paper covers surrounded hand-illustrated pages, filled with sentiments such as "I like school. I like the swings. The swings are fun."

"Do you see what I did at school today?"

I carefully flipped through her epic. "You did a good job."

"I know. But when I gave it to Mrs. T., she didn't give me a check!"

"What?"

"You said we don't write for free in our family! I wrote that whole book, and now I want some money!"

One's vocabulary can make parenting difficult. For a few years, we lived in a less than perfect neighborhood, and the language that floated around was distinctly not children-friendly. Worse, I've been known to use language that would make a sailor leave the room in horror. I've been trying to curb the habit, but occasionally words slip through.

So I explained to the girls that there are swear words, but that there is an appropriate time and place for them. Just drop a heavy can of juice on your toe? An expletive might be in order. Miss out on the last brownie at the church social? Not the time for profanity.

This seemed to work really well until the day Harmony just did not want to go to school. We had a royal battle of the wills, and as the possessor of the older, bigger will, I won. Harmony was standing in the driveway waiting for the bus, tears streaming down her face.

When the bus arrived, I explained to the driver that Harmony had had a really rough morning.

"That's okay," he replied. "Things will get better, won't they, Harmony?"

She glared at him with all the angry disdain a six-year-old can muster. "The hell they will!" she snapped, before stomping back to her seat. I guess I'll have to revise my appropriate profanity-location lecture to cover school-bus etiquette.

Knowing you have to watch your words when you speak directly to the children is one thing, but dealing with what they overhear and interpret is something else entirely. I'd been chatting on the phone with a slightly older female friend who'd been having some medical problems.

The next day I received a phone call from the school nurse. She was barely able to control her laughter.

"Mrs. Potts? I have Harmony in here. I think you should know she's not feeling well."

"What's the matter?"

"First she's hot," the nurse said, stifling a giggle. "Then she's cold. She's tired. She's in a horrible mood." The nurse paused for a moment. "But Harmony knows what the problem is. Apparently, she has menopause."

Fortunately my youngest doesn't have quite the same flair for picking up adult vocabulary, but she does have her own unique comprehension and interpretation skills. Baby Nadia has developed a deep and abiding fascination with the cat box. There's nothing more interesting, apparently, than sitting in the gravel and playing with what's contained therein.

Time after time after time, we took Nadia out of the cat box. "No, Nadia," I'd say, "That's yucky. That's where the kitties go potty. It's all poop and pee."

Then, of course, it came time to potty train Nadia. She was running around sans diaper, in the hopes that I could catch her before she had an accident and get her to sit on the potty in time.

So when she started to dance around, shifting from foot to foot, I asked her, "Nadia, do you have to go potty?"

Realization dawned in her eyes, and her whole face lit up. Encouraged, I started to reach for her, but she squirmed out of my grasp and ran, just as fast as her little legs would carry her, right for the cat box.

She may not be potty trained yet, but at least she's housebroken.

• • • • •

Cynthia Potts is a full-time freelance writer, who does her very best to balance professional word slinging with raising two incredibly smart, beautiful, and energetic daughters. If she has any free time, she enjoys spending it sleeping like a rock or luxuriating in a bath without any Barbies, toy trucks, or plastic dinosaurs.

The Purple Pee

By Lisa Harsch

One Friday this last fall my six-year-old son, Jacob, and my three-year-old daughter, Chloe, were playing in the yard while my husband and I were working in the garage. Chloe came into the garage to show me the pretty red berries she'd found.

I immediately freaked. "You didn't eat them, did you?" She insisted she hadn't, but I think I scared her and she wouldn't tell me. I asked my son, who said he didn't know.

I told Chloe she could get really sick if she ate things she found outside and I would have to take her to the hospital. She seemed to understand but I still wasn't really sure if she had eaten them or not. After all, this is the girl who eats chewed bubble gum that she finds on the sidewalk. Oh, and there was that time she found the bird's egg. Yuck!

But the night went on and she was fine, though the next morning Chloe woke up hysterical with a tummy ache. It was Saturday and I had to work; my husband was gone and Mom was to take the kids for the day. I was the only manager on duty that day and there would be no way to find a replacement on the weekend. What could I do? My husband's a contractor and if he doesn't work, he doesn't get paid.

I did the motherly things, asking "Where does it hurt?" and "Are you hungry?" and feeling her to see if she was warm or if her tummy was hard or hurt to touch. She didn't seem to have a fever or any signs of the flu and none of her friends or classmates had been sick. I still suspected the berries.

Finally, I got exasperated. *"Did you eat those berries???* I told you not to eat them!" She insisted she hadn't. "Do you have to poop?" No, she didn't. I put her in a warm bath and gave her some Pepto-Bismol.

She got out and lay down for a little while, and fell asleep. She seemed to feel better when she got up, so I packed the kids up, and took them to my mom's. I explained to my mom that Chloe had had a tummy ache earlier but was doing fine now. All seemed well and I made it to work.

Then the call came. Chloe was moaning and groaning about how much her tummy hurt. She had fallen asleep but was still moaning. And she had purple pee.

Purple pee? There was no fever, but I had told my mom about the berries.

Purple pee? Do you mean red or pink? "Do you think she has a urinary tract infection?" my mom asked. Not if it was purple! "Are you sure it was purple?" Yes. "Could it have been the Pepto-Bismol?" I immediately got off the phone, went down to the nurses' station at work, and looked in the med interaction book at Pepto-Bismol. No purple pee.

I asked the nurses and they had never heard of purple pee. I went back to my office and called the doctors' office and told a nurse what had happened. They said Pepto-Bismol could not cause purple pee, and a doctor could call me back.

The call came within minutes and they told me to bring her to Children's ER. Oh, and bring a sample of the berries; then they could run tests and see if they were toxic or not.

Great. I really had no clue where these berries were. I frantically called my husband and told him he needed to get the berries, pick Chloe up, and take her to the ER. In the meantime I called my mom and asked how Chloe was doing and told her my husband was on his way.

She hesitated: "I talked to your dad and he put Rust-o-leum in the toilet and it must have reacted with her pee."

I didn't know whether to laugh or wring their necks. I had just spent an hour on the phone during our busiest time feeling guilty about leaving Chloe, frantic that she was really sick, and wondering what I was going to do about work. At least Chloe was okay. The moral of the story is know your berries, don't scare your kids so they won't tell you the truth, and, most important, ask your parents how they clean the toilet.

● ● ● ● ●

Lisa Harsch is a wife and mother of two, Jacob (6½) and Chloe (4). She is director of dining services at Luther Manor. She and her husband, Chad, have been married almost eight years and own a small construction business.

Mom Drops the Bomb

By Erica R. Lewandowski

It was a cold winter day and I was yearning to shop. Now, at seventeen months, my daughter was not a big fan of shopping, but I was armed and ready. She was fresh from a nap; I had packed snacks, toys, and, as a back up, I had my cell phone and car keys (they could always be counted on for at least a half-hour of entertainment). I was raring to go, planning to make the most of the two hours I thought I could squeak out of her. I really needed shampoo, a new top, and well, shoes—don't we all need shoes?

I knew I was in for trouble the minute my daughter's bottom hit the seat of the stroller—let's just say it didn't stay there for long. She started what I've termed the alligator roll—think big green monster thrashing about in the water trying to rip its prey limb from limb. My daughter was doing the 24-pound, red-headed imp version, and it's not cute. Undaunted, I gave her a pack of raisins and headed in. I *really* needed retail therapy.

Next came the high-pitched cry. The one that makes everyone look your way to see what horrible thing you must be doing to your child. The one that reverberates off all the walls of the stores and amplifies if the stroller stops moving. The one that you know means trouble and you had better seek the shelter of the car immediately. But the shoe department called. I gave my daughter my car keys and pressed on.

My daughter's last-ditch effort for freedom came as I attempted to try on a pair of new spring sandals. She too had decided that winter apparel was no longer in fashion and had begun to remove hers piece by piece. While her cries escalated, off came her shoes and socks, soon followed by her coat and shirt. As I scampered around the store trying to collect our belongings and re-dress my angry, squirming, wailing child, it became apparent that this wasn't going to work.

Thirty minutes into shopping, it was all over—my trip, that is. My daughter had had enough, despite the kind attempt by the saleslady making cutesy faces (she promptly had a fistful of raisins chucked her way), the well-intentioned grandmother holding the elevator for us (boy, did she regret that), and the unsuspecting gentleman who had a pink size-five sneaker bounce off his leg as he strolled by.

What happened next I am not proud of—I became *that* mom. You know, the one who is trying to discipline her child in a too-loud voice and is getting nowhere. The one who is frantically trying to get her child to "*Sit down*, please, *sit down*," with no success, as she hands her child anything, *anything* at all that might placate her for the briefest moment. The one who has earned the disapproval of mothers with angelic

• •

children who watch with a look of scorn and distain . . . as if their kids have NEVER done it!

We both reached the car tearful, sweaty, and half dressed—my daughter missing her socks, shoes, coat, and half of her shirt. Overheated from toddler-wrangling, I had shed my coat and sweatshirt. I strapped her into her car seat, despite a renewed wave of protests, and informed her that "Mommy is mad, really mad. All Mommy wanted was to go shopping for a little bit. Don't you realize how little Mommy asks from you? You can sit in your seat and cry all the way home if you want. Mommy's done!" A startled look crossed my daughter's face. She had never seen me like this, and I had never raised my voice at her before. Out came the quivering bottom lip, and the waterworks really began—for both of us. I felt so awful, a bad-mommy moment, and little did I know that it was about to get worse.

I drove into traffic, fighting the lunch rush entering the mall. My guilt soon turned into road rage as I waited for a distracted driver on a cell phone in front of us to move at a green light. I had reached my emotional melting point for the day— "What the f*#&," I exclaimed, as I flashed him the appropriate hand gesture. "Get off the phone and drive!"

Fortunately, we began to inch forward and soon we were on our way home. As we pulled away, leaving the scene of the "crime," I began to feel my frustration and anger ebb away . . . I mean, after all, everyone probably has a day like that with their kids every once in a while, right? My daughter was still

• •

the angelic cherub she'd been at breakfast—this whole experience was just a fluke.

"F*#&," a tiny voice from the backseat twittered, "F*#&, f*#&, f*#&!" I gasped in horror, was I really hearing what I thought I was hearing? "F*#&!" I heard again, this time with gusto, as I turned to see my daughter flip me the bird with a smile on her face. A wave of panic washed over me—what had I done? Had I actually taught my daughter the f-bomb? Where was my self-control, where was the loving and positive role model I had planned to be for my child? Is she going to keep saying it? Is there any way I can blame this on her father?

I willed the panic away and drove on in silence, stealing peeks at my daughter in the rearview mirror. She seemed to have abandoned the temper tantrums and profanity, and for the moment, was happily munching away on a stowaway cracker she'd discovered in the depths of her car seat. Our life seemed to have returned to normal, and I was just going to have to deal with what had happened. I was just going to go home and forget that this whole day had even happened. We'd start fresh tomorrow, or after her afternoon nap, anyway. The f-bomb was nowhere to be heard—for the time being anyway.

• • • • •

Erica R. Lewandowski left her career as an environmental scientist to stay home and raise her only child, Olivia. After a long day of toddler-wrangling, she enjoys spending time with her husband, Mike. She resides in Milwaukee, Wisconsin.

Talking Turkey

By K.V. Norgard

When my daughter was two years old, she had delayed speech and was still struggling to speak even the simplest words. Her pediatrician recommended delaying speech therapy until she'd reached the age of three and was ready to enter preschool. I had read every book on the market on early-childhood development, but nothing I tried seemed to work. She could produce only the most basic sounds that were incomprehensible to everyone, except me.

On Thanksgiving morning, she sat in her highchair watching me as I prepared the turkey. As I endeavored to fit the oversized roasting pan into our undersized oven, I let fly every obscenity I generally reserve for driving in rush-hour traffic.

At dinner that evening, with my very proper in-laws in attendance, the topic of my daughter's delayed speech came up. They delighted in accusing me of not doing all that was necessary to correct the problem. If I was a better mother, they implied, she would be speaking like any other child of two. To convince them that I was doing all that I could to advance her language skills, I coaxed her to speak. At one point, my daughter pointed toward the platter and demanded, "Mo . . . mo," meaning that she desired another helping of turkey.

"What would you like more of, sweetheart?" I asked, encouraging her to elaborate as best she could.

With perfect enunciation, she said, "More damn bird!"

Much to my relief, my in-laws laughed. My daughter was so excited by the response her new vocabulary created, that she repeated the phrase throughout the rest of the meal. That was, by far, the most memorable Thanksgiving our family ever celebrated.

• • • • •

K. V. Norgard leads a life of obscurity in California as an underappreciated homemaker and mother of a teenage daughter. She moonlights as an Internet fan fiction writer, and has won awards for her humor. She is currently at work on her first original novel.

Beyond the Books

By Vanessa Lindores—Farah

"**P**oop again, Mommy, so I can watch!" This from my outraged two-and-a-half-year-old as I step out of the bathroom. He doesn't like to be left out of anything. I dream of turning around and locking myself in again—for a long time. But I know there will be screaming and pathetic clawing at the door. I want to say "You can't talk to me like that. I have a master's degree, you know! I went to university for, like, seven years!" Instead I hear myself trying to negotiate. "How about if I pee instead? Would that be okay?"

What has happened to me? Don't get me wrong, I knew parenting wouldn't always be easy. I'm a youngest child and didn't have much exposure to kids growing up so I knew there would be a lot for me to learn. But I wasn't prepared for how truly bizarre raising two young children could get. And education doesn't help one bit, at least not the kind I have. When I got an A on Professor Calvet's international finance final in the second year of my M.B.A., I really believed there was nothing I couldn't figure out if I tried hard enough. Learning how to calculate currency swaps and options wasn't easy for me, but fully comprehending my children has me stumped so far.

It's not that I'm not trying. After spending so many years in school, I'm doing what all good students do. I'm reading books—lots of them. I'm not sure how much good they do. I suppose they do give me more insight into how children think and perceive the world. And their very existence reassures me. If parenting were simple, there wouldn't be a gazillion books on the subject. So that helps. So far though, I haven't found direct references to some of the weirder things I've faced.

Like when my son asked "Mommy, can I put my car in your boobs?" I mean, how does one respond to something like that? "No," just doesn't seem to cut it. I guess you have to extrapolate. Through my extensive research I have learned that you are supposed to offer a lot of nonjudgmental praise and encourage independent thinking. So maybe it should be "No, but you sure have managed to narrow down what will very likely be key long-term interests early in life. Well done!"

I'm sure you can over-think and worry too much about things when it comes to parenting. Maybe I shouldn't be so concerned that I only just learned the danger of negatively labeling your "spirited" child. Turns out referring to your child as "The Destroyer" may not be great for the self-esteem. Oops. Okay, he's now officially "The Reverse Engineer."

The danger of intellectualizing too much about raising the perfectly balanced, self-confident, independent-thinking, artistic, creative, yet scientific-minded individual is that every situation seems to take on an exaggerated importance. My mind started racing when my son asked "When I'm fully potty-trained, can I get a big brother?" Where do I begin? Is this a chance to discourage rewards-based motivation? Or should I be doing a science lesson on the law of time? Maybe it's an opportunity to talk about where babies come from?

With all of the reading I've done and all of my good intentions I'm a little ashamed to admit that my response could have come directly from the mouth of my dear late mother, who as far as I know didn't read any books on child rearing.

I said, "We'll see."

• • • • •

Vanessa Lindores-Farah is a full-time mom of two young children. She has an undergraduate degree in geography and a master's in international business. In her professional life she has worked in public policy, and environmental and land planning. Raised in Ottawa, Canada, she now lives in California with her husband and children.

Belly Buttonholed

By Judy Ford

I was raised in a conservative household in a small, southern-Idaho town by a mother who detested exercise and a father who was a strict Nazarene. Growing up I dreamed of becoming a dancer. Our next-door neighbor, Mimi Anderson, gave tap lessons to a handful of local girls in her basement on Tuesday evenings. I loved the shine of the black leather Mary Janes and the sound of shuffle steps across a wood floor, but when I asked my parents if I could join the class, they resounded, "Absolutely not!"

Our Nazarene church forbade such forms of expression. Several years later I presented my mother with another request. I asked her if I could get my ears pierced. She told me to ask my father. I asked my dad and he said, "If God wanted you to wear earrings you would have been born with holes in your ears."

To this day I still dream of tapping, only now I am filled with nearly fifty long years of excuses—too old, too out of shape, too uncoordinated—as to why I cannot take a dance class. Fifty years is a lot to sort through. And although I did eventually get my ears pierced it was not done professionally. Instead a college sorority sister used ice cubes to numb me then jammed a darning needle through my lobes. She inadvertently placed the holes too low leaving me unable to wear the heavy, dangling earrings that were the reason I wanted to get my ears pierced in the first place.

Before Amanda was even born I vowed to teach her differently than my parents had taught me. I wanted my daughter to feel comfortable in her body, to find joy in swinging her arms and picking up her feet. So when I saw an advertisement for a local gymnastics studio offering "play-filled exercise" for children, I knew we had to give it a try.

From day one Amanda was in bliss. The ease with which she somersaulted, and hung from monkey bars, and swayed her hips to the music of the tiny ukulele that the instructor played at the end of class was proof that I had made the right choice.

Amanda continued to take gymnastics classes once a week for nearly ten years. During that time she also fell in love with swimming, spending so much time at the city pool that her fingertips became wrinkled like prunes and her blonde hair tinted chlorine green. As mothers we are called upon daily to make decisions for our children, to guide and help them navigate this complicated world in which we live. Sometimes these decisions are easy. Answering teenaged Amanda when she bounded into the kitchen two weeks before her fourteenth birthday wearing a bright pink bikini and asked, "Can I get my bellybutton pierced?" was difficult.

Maybe it seems like no big deal and maybe I seem old-fashioned for even batting an eyelash at the question. Piercings, tattoos, and other forms of personal expression are commonplace these days, but I must admit that my first thought upon hearing my daughter's request was, "Are you insane? Under absolutely no circumstances am I letting you pierce your bellybutton."

I kept this initial response to myself, however, having learned early on that the best way to address hot topics with Amanda is with a light heart. Instead of polarizing the situation with a flat-out, "No way!" I said instead, "We'll see," hoping she would forget about the belly ring by morning.

Amanda did not forget. Over the next several days she repeated her question over and over: "Can I get my bellybutton pierced?" And each time I responded like a broken record, "We'll see. We'll see."

Quickly Amanda's tone grew from hopeful yet casual to feverish and demanding. She begged. She pleaded. She talked circles around me.

"What's the big deal?" she wanted to know. "It's not like I'm piercing my eyebrow or nose. It's my stomach. Nobody will even see it."

After five days of these seemingly nonstop bellybutton inquisitions, my mind was on spin cycle. As I tried to fall asleep that night, another question popped into my mind. "What are you afraid of, Judy?" I had to ask myself.

The question stopped my breath for a moment. What was I afraid of? I began making a mental list of my fears. I was afraid that Amanda's desire to pierce her bellybutton was proof that my sweet daughter was turning into a "bad kid." I imagined a ring in Amanda's navel would lead to all sorts of undesirable behavior like bootlegging beer outside seedy convenience stores and having unprotected sex with sweet-talking older boys in the back seats of their cars. I was afraid that Amanda's classmates, in hopes of persuading their own mothers to endorse body piercing, would run home shouting, "Amanda's mom let her do it!" I was afraid of those mothers calling me, enraged, yelling, "What were you thinking?" I was afraid of what my own mother would have to say. I was afraid I would be called careless, irresponsible and blind.

Then I thought back to my own adolescence and remembered how I had never done anything wild as a girl. The one impetuous thing I did was write "Elvis" in red lipstick on the wallpaper in the bathroom of the only movie theater in our town. After the owner called my mother, she cried hysterically for hours about how I had ruined my father's reputation as the town banker. I begged my mom not to tell my dad and she said that she wouldn't on the condition that I "shaped up" and began "acting like a lady" from that point on.

I finally decided to let Amanda get her bellybutton pierced, because way down in the deepest recesses of my gut where instinct resides I knew that a small ring through the navel was not enough to spoil the core of my loving, thoughtful, intelligent daughter. I figured that just as I had helped teach Amanda to love her body by enrolling her in gymnastics classes as a toddler, I could also teach her to embrace her wild yearnings while remaining a responsible, kind, thriving human being.

Thus on the day of her fourteenth birthday—with my own mother's "You're giving her what for her birthday?" still ringing in my mind—I drove Amanda downtown where a man covered in tattoos used a three-inch needle to put a small silver ring through her bellybutton. Of course I was nervous during it all, but when it was finished and I saw the smile on Amanda's face, I relaxed.

Today, at twenty-six Amanda no longer has a hole in her navel. She removed it ten years ago, just three weeks after her sixteenth birthday. Next month my darling daughter will catch a plane and fly over 2,000 miles away to move in with a man who is thirteen years her senior and whom she has only known for six months. Of course I am nervous. I am afraid that she will get homesick, that she will get lost in a strange, new city, that the relationship between her and this man will fall apart, that she will return home dejected and brokenhearted. Once again, however, I must trust my purest instinct that tells me to support my daughter's desire for adventure. Holes in bellybuttons and cracks in hearts, while painful at first, heal faster and cause less damage than the weight of unfilled longings and years spent wondering, "What if?"

It is never easy to know the "best" way to raise a child. But when we are truly concerned for the well-being of our little ones we will rise above our own ridiculous fears and do better than what was done for us.

If we are lucky, our children will take the best of us, improve on it, and become better.

• • • • •

Judy Ford, L.C.S.W., is a nationally recognized family therapist, author, and mother. She is the author of the bestselling *Wonderful Ways to Love a Child,* and *Wonderful Ways to Love a Teen.* Her media appearances include: Oprah, CNN, and National Public Radio. For more information visit: *www. judyford.com.*

Blessing in Disguise

BY KAREN Y. OZOLNIEKS

"Mom, don't freak out but I've had an accident." These are words that strike terror in the heart of a parent with a teenage driver.

The change had happened so fast. Our polite, respectful little girl had turned into a teenager with a vengeance. This phase in our lives seemed to coincide with when she started driving. We were so proud when we presented her with that car. True, it was older than she was, but it was a car. The all-American symbol of freedom and independence.

That was when the turmoil began. At times I feel like our family must be the most dysfunctional family on the planet. I've often wondered what made me think I could raise a child into a well-adjusted adult. Maybe I should have stuck to dogs and cats. Our therapist says it's normal adolescent stuff. My husband says it's payback time for the things we put our parents through. I think she's trying to kill me with worry.

When there are problems with my daughter my first instinct is usually to blame myself. I start thinking things like, "Maybe

I was too hard on her." "Maybe I was too easy on her." "Maybe I didn't spend enough time with her." It's even easier to blame her father, thinking things like, "He should have been a better role model."

My husband and I keep telling each other, "We have to stick together. We must be consistent. We have to back each other up." However, this can be difficult when you're up against someone whose strategy seems to be divide and conquer.

I remember when she used to be glad to see me. When I used to sneak out the door so I could do the weekly grocery shopping alone in peace. She was such a sweet, vivacious, uncorrupted soul. Now I rarely see her. She's either not at home, or if she is home, she's holed up in her room.

For everyone who has a teen or will one day have a teen, here's what I've learned so far:

Sometimes kids just do things and it's not anybody's fault but their own. Pray a lot. I pray to all the Gods to make sure I've covered all the bases.

Most families are dysfunctional in their own way. Some are more dysfunctional than others but even those that appear to be well-adjusted have problems.

Most of all, in the midst of the anger and the feelings of betrayal, make sure they know you will always love them and only want what is best for them. Because if you give up on them, they will surely give up on themselves.

Somehow our daughter managed to wrap her little car around a cement telephone pole and walk away without a scratch. The car was totaled but fortunately no one was hurt. However the accident was the culmination of a downward spiral that included failing grades, sneaking out of the house at night, skipping school, and associating with people of questionable character.

Losing the car turned out to be a good thing. She inadvertently did for herself what her father and I didn't have the courage to do for her. It allowed us to reel her in and take back some of the freedom we had granted her. Just because the State of Florida says sixteen-year-olds are ready for more responsibility doesn't necessarily mean all of them are. What could have been a tragedy turned out to be a blessing.

• • • • •

Karen Y. Ozolnieks is a technical writer for a software company in Lake Mary, Florida. Karen attended the University of Central Florida and has degrees in political science and computer programming. Karen is a native Floridian and currently resides in Oviedo with her family. Her hobbies include buying and selling antiques.

Mine for a Day

By Sheri McGregor

Having given my teenage daughter her medicine and fluffed up her pillows, I stand in the doorway. Her cheeks are flushed, the small wisps of hair near her forehead damp with perspiration so they curl all around her forehead. Today, she looks so young I can hardly believe she's the same long-legged, maturing beauty that turns heads everywhere we go.

"Can I get you anything else?" I step close to palm her moist forehead again, relieved that her skin is cool to the touch. She's much better today—and I feel lucky to have her to myself. This morning, there was no nagging her out of bed and rushing her off to school, off to her friends, basketball practice, algebra homework, and Spanish study she rolls off her tongue like she was born to the language. No stopping in the doorway, knowing she wasn't really sick, but letting her stay home anyway—which I sometimes do. She really is ill.

"How about I make you a smoothie?" I ask, relishing the immediate upward tilt of her mouth, and the way her soft brown eyes light. "Be right back."

As I walk up the hall toward the kitchen, sadness or gladness lodges in the back of my throat. It's as if I've stepped back in time, as if I'm the one lying there in bed and my mother the one here heading into the kitchen.

When I was about my daughter's age, I contracted strep throat so severely that pus pockets sprouted like popcorn from my tonsils. My throat raw, every swallow cut like a knife. Not wanting to miss out on anything, I hid the illness from my mother. I continued seeing my boyfriend, and carrying on with school activities until I was so sick all I could do was vomit and cry. My mother draped a sweater over my shoulders and carted me off to the doctor.

In his office, she only shrugged and apologized when he looked at her in accusatory horror and asked, "Why did you wait so long to bring her in?"

And never once did my mother scold me for not telling her sooner.

At home, she tucked me into bed for a week, cheerfully, quietly presiding over me around the clock. She dutifully brought my medicine, and tried to entice me to eat with small portions of soft foods she cooked specially for me. By the eighth day, I was well enough to swallow real food and speak.

My mother took my plate. "In a couple of days, you'll have to go back to school," she said, her smile odd, not quite matching her eyes. "You'll be back to everything."

I grinned, thinking of my boyfriend. "I can't wait to see Craig." It would be good to get back to all my friends. Yet, with

• •

her standing there looking down at me, something sad lodged deep in the pit of my stomach. I wanted to be well, but I'd miss this time with my mother.

It was always like this. Once, when I was seven, I'd cried for no reason about going to school. "Just stay home," my mother said, just the way I have allowed my daughter to occasionally linger in bed.

Suddenly, on that recovering-from-strep-throat day, my mother leaned down and kissed me on the cheek. She hugged me so tightly I thought I'd burst.

"Gosh, Mom," I protested, not quite able to admit how comforted I felt by her embrace.

"You're still my baby," she said, heading quickly away. In the doorway, she stopped and turned to look at me, her eyes red-rimmed. She smiled. "I'll bring you some juice." A moment later, she returned with purple grape juice in a Scooby Doo jelly-jar glass with a flexible straw.

"Thanks," I said, as she started to leave. And then, because I couldn't stand for her to go, I called, "Momma, can't you sit with me for a while?" I patted the bed.

She laughed, coming back to perch beside me, her soft brown eyes full of love. My friends would be there in a few days, and I looked forward to getting back to my busy teenage life. But just then, all I needed was my momma, and some cold juice in a glass with a flexible straw.

Now, all these years later, the fuzzy memory made me smile as I fixed my own teenage daughter a yogurt and fresh blueberry smoothie. I rifled around in the cupboard for a minute, joyful when I found a box of flexible straws where I'd stashed them last time one of the kids was sick, or needed a little extra love. Ignoring the business phone line when it rang, I extended the accordion section and bent it just so for drinking. Then I deliver it to my daughter.

When she smiles and pats the bed for me to sit, I think how lucky I am to have her all to myself. In a few days, she'll be back to basketball and all her friends. And that's only the beginning. In a few short years, she'll be on with her adult life. But right now, what she needs most is her momma's love, all mixed up in a cold smoothie presented with a flexible straw.

• • • • •

Sheri McGregor writes a diverse mix of fiction and nonfiction books and shorts. Corporate writing includes medical/psychology materials, such as the recent "Teen Wellness Kit" she authored for Families for Depression Awareness. Her latest book, *60 Hikes Within 60 Miles: San Diego* (*www.SanDiego Hikes.com*) combines her love of nature and words.

Gentle Guidance

By Celeste Carter Murphy

My husband was feeding my daughter one day and was frustrated because she wouldn't eat. He was worried that she wasn't getting enough vegetables so he tried to shove the spoon into her mouth. Just a toddler, she pushed his hand away, looked at him firmly and said, "Don't force!" My husband looked stunned and we both cracked up laughing. That was a foreshadowing of what was to come. It was also exactly as I raised her to be.

I've always viewed my mothering role as similar to a guide's. My job is to show my children the world and let them choose their own path. So, I've let them experiment with all of the typical childhood things: gymnastics, music lessons, art classes . . . you know the list goes on and on. Our son, Declan, soaks up every opportunity that comes along. Jillian, however, never really latched on to anything. In theory her independence seems like a terrific quality. For a parent, it's always hard to remember that this outcome is intentional.

The children in our play group were all perfect and highly intelligent, according to their parents. The little Kristins and Connors were reading by the age of three and playing their first piano concert at four. Now, I know this probably sounds like I was jealous. Darn right I was. I wasn't at all disappointed that Jillian would rather build nests out of sticks at the playground than learn how to cartwheel on a balance beam. I was disappointed that I hadn't urged her to do so. I felt like I was failing as her guide. I wasn't empowering her to be all that she could be. I didn't force.

At about twenty months of age, an age when most little girls are still being dressed in adorable outfits with matching accessories, Jillian insisted on dressing herself. She painstakingly sorted through her clothes to put outfits together. Once, my husband came home, and as he drove up, he thought he saw a stranger playing outside of our home, as she was far fatter than our daughter. It was Jillian in eleven of her prettiest dresses. That was probably her record for layers, but she usually wore at least four outfits all at once. A friend once said that her own mother would "just die" if she let her daughter dress this way. What a sad way to die.

As Jillian grew I continued to try to gently guide her. But still, I got hung up on the "look what my kid can do" comparison train. I spent too much money on Montessori preschool and kindergarten. Thinking that this approach would nurture Jillian's spirit, lead to her acceptance at an Ivy League college and guarantee her success in life. Fortunately the Montessori approach is accepting of allowing children to follow their own path, but it wasn't until she went to public school that she really began to shine. I could have saved our family a lot of money.

During her elementary-school years gentle leadership began to pay off. Jillian was and still is a focused student. She became interested in birds and read everything she could find about them. Staying true to my job description as guide I searched for opportunities for her to explore her interest further. I took her on bird walks with the local bird club, visited the birds-of-prey rescue center and even sent her to birding camp one summer. She was really into it. By age thirteen she had participated in everything she could. Adults were consulting her with their bird questions. She then decided that what she really wanted was to learn to be a falconer. But law required that she wait until she was seventeen. So I took a bit of a break as her guide to the world of birding. Without opportunities, she lost interest. My loss was greater. I watched a focused, intelligent nature lover turn into a teenager.

Now she is focused on typical teenage things such as music and clothes. Her outfits are again extreme. Her hair is purple and her wardrobe consists of one color—black. Some parents ask me why I allow her to dress this way. Their children are involved in sports, and shopping at Abercrombie & Fitch. Do I have a choice? Not without force. I have to constantly remind myself of my belief that in the end using gentle guidance will enable my children to develop into the people they were meant to be. Through gentle guidance I will show them the world. By

• •

choosing their own path they will build self-esteem and self-respect.

I've had open and frank discussions with my children about tough issues such as sex, drugs, and peer pressure. Jillian has become a leader among her friends. She dresses radically but her message is clear—she respects herself, excels in school, and looks out for her friends when they appear to be headed for trouble.

I'm hoping that gentle guidance can get me through the teenage years. I always worry that I should rule with a stronger hand during this time. But I remind myself that through all of the ups and downs of the early years gentle leading has always worked in the long run. When I look at my children beyond the moment I see that they are developing into caring, confident people. And it doesn't matter if they don't attend prestigious universities or have high-power jobs earning salaries with a lot of commas. The only thing that really carries any weight is that they are happy and pass that on to their own children. But I have to admit that I worry that I'm not doing enough. So I take Jillian's advice, "Don't force!"

• • • • •

Celeste Carter Murphy lives in Colorado with her menagerie that includes one husband, one teenage daughter, a preteen son, two cats, and one dog. The impending arrival of another daughter will bring more exciting parenting challenges. In her spare time Ms. Murphy writes short fiction and articles on consumer issues.

Mom's Angry Face

By Karen McMillen

I had waited until my mid-thirties to become a mother, and like everyone, had very high expectations for myself. I would be the über-mother: able to negotiate any and all difficult child-rearing situations with ease and grace, building the most loving of mother-child relationships.

. . . Or at the very least, I would make none of the mistakes that I felt my mother had made with me. Mom was angry a lot. She didn't seem to have much fun raising two embattled girls, mostly on her own. My sister and I still joke about Mom's "Angry Face"—the bulging eyes, the gnashing teeth, the death-grip on the back of your neck. That, I vowed, would never be me. I'd never had a problem with anger.

Then I had my first child.

He was a beautiful little bundle of intensity, with emotions that completely trumped his size. At first it was amusing to see his little face all scrunched up in anger and to encounter his acts of pint-sized defiance. Then it was exhausting. I often laid awake at night worrying about what I had in store for me when he reached adolescence, given that his will at the age of two already completely outstripped mine. By the time he was sixteen months old, all of my notions about über-motherhood had flown out the window and I was hanging on by my fingernails, just hoping that we would both survive the next sixteen years without a visit from the Department of Social Services.

As a mother I have experienced rage that I never knew could exist in an otherwise sane person—all directed toward someone less than three feet tall. Someone who in a few short years has managed to discover and master the art of manipulating every button I never knew I had. I have taken my mother's Angry Face to a whole new level; in fact, I'm sure that there was at least one time when actual steam came out of my ears.

I understood the logic of corporal punishment; it may not be a very healthy tool for teaching the child, but, *oh*, what a release for the parent! It often takes every ounce of restraint I have not to hit my son, especially when he is hitting, kicking, and biting me. The best alternative I can muster most of the time is to shout: "Mommy needs a time-out!" and lock myself in a room. I suspect that this takes its own kind of emotional toll on my son, but it's the best I can do.

I have discovered that yelling is my release. *"Put that down this instant!" "I said do* not *throw things in the house!" "Never, never kick the cat!"* I had no idea just how loud I could be, and I'm not proud of it. Before we had our son, we moved from a tiny condo in the city to a house on what felt like an expansive quarter-acre lot. Given the decibels I can reach when my son and I lock horns, I felt sure that the condo association would throw us out by his first birthday, and frankly, I'm kind of wishing we had held out for a solid acre lot. There are days when I'm afraid to meet my neighbors in the street.

I recently bought my toddler a book about a little girl named Sophie who gets so mad sometimes that she is like a volcano, ready to explode (*When Sophie Gets Angry, Very, Very Angry*, by Molly Bang). He related to it instantly, though I'm not sure whether the connection came from his experience of his own toddler-sized rage, or of the seismic anger of his mother.

For a long time I suffered mightily. I felt that my failings as a parent—and alas, developed so early!—were unique. Then I began to hear whisperings from other mothers.

At a play date with several other toddlers, one mom (whom I had never taken much of a shine to) was talking about a particularly hard day she and her daughter had recently had: "It's mind-blowing," she said. "I never used to get this mad at any of my coworkers!" I looked at this woman anew and began to feel the stirrings of a powerful kinship. She continued: "It seems like every day I get so mad that I have to close my eyes and count to ten to try to calm myself down. Then she starts in: 'Mommy, why are you counting?' Aaaargh!"

Then there was my perfect friend, who works forty-hour weeks as a "part-time" lawyer, yet still finds time to make bonbons from scratch and create flower-shaped windmills with her children. She once described how merely asking her three-year-old to put on her shoes degenerated to the point where, and I quote: "If someone had handed me a stick, I would have hit her. Honestly," she said, "I can't quit my job and stay home full-time. They would lock me up and take my children!"

And then there was the time that after a particularly Bad, Bad Day, I left our little devil child in the care of his father and escaped to the mall. In the elevator to the parking garage, I squeezed in with a mom and dad and their two young children. Their oldest was having a whopper of a meltdown, and I kept trying to meet the parents' eyes to offer them a sympathetic glance. But they were locked in their own embattled world, and the mother, after repeatedly hissing at her son to *knock it off,* turned to the father and said, "I swear I'm going to kill him in about four minutes." The father, glancing my way, said, "Shhhhh." And then the mother turned on him: "Don't *shush me!*"

I walked out of the elevator feeling lighter than I had in days.

• • • • •

Karen McMillen is Joe's mom, a producer of videos for museums, television, and other educational entities, and a freelance writer living in the Boston area.

Testing Boundaries

By Meaghan McKenna-Porcelly

When my son began to bite other kids at eighteen months old, at first I tried to be firm and redirect his behavior to something else. When it really came down to it, I just couldn't accept that my little boy was doing anything wrong, despite the fact that through his actions he was making other kids, other moms, and even me completely miserable.

Nobody likes a bully. I feared that my son was destined to be a menace to society and that he would never make any friends. Now I have more perspective. I don't think that my son, even when he was going around sinking his teeth into whatever other child he could find, understood enough to deliberately torment the other babies. Being unable to express himself verbally, he was looking for a way to communicate with the people around him, and of course, he was testing the boundaries of what is right and what is wrong. Still, he was biting—and sometimes hitting, and kicking, or pinching—and it was my job as his mother to correct his behavior. But I simply could not figure out how to do it. I tried redirecting him to play with something else, scolding him firmly, and even resorted to just up and leaving wherever we were and taking him home. I experimented with giving him time-out, only to have to struggle with him while he fought his way out of the time-out chair. That little guy was going to do whatever he wanted, whenever he wanted.

This was completely frustrating not only to me, but to the other mothers whose children were on the receiving end of these awkward exchanges. I have to say that I have now had the experience of being the mother of the tormenter and of the tormented, and I would prefer my child to be the victim of those toddler-aged squabbles any day. I got unsolicited advice from every direction—I was told that I should spank, that I should shout, and that I should lock him in a room. I was really beginning to doubt myself as a parent. As a young, first-time mom, I was struggling against my instincts. I tried spanking him, but it was more painful to me than it was motivational to him.

As time went on, though, my relationship with my little boy actually started to deteriorate. I started to feel helpless, and convinced that his behavior as just a toddler was going to somehow significantly affect the way he was going to live for the rest of his life.

I knew nobody would like my son or me, because I was a bad mom. I wasn't sure I wanted to go anywhere.

It took the advice of a wonderful mother and a kind friend to get us through what turned out to be only a passing phase. Her own son had been through the same experience and she had lived to tell about it. She pulled me aside one particularly trying day and explained, "You are his mother. Nobody else can take better care of him, nobody else will love him more, and nobody else knows what is best for him. You are his number-one advocate and should stick by him through thick and thin."

For a brief moment I felt totally shamed by what she had said, and I wondered how I could have been so silly and naive. It was plain and simple what I had to do—I planted my two heels firmly in the ground, took my little boy by the hand, and moved on. There was no need for books, more advice, or guilt. I felt a weight lift off my shoulders, and the relationship between my son and myself improved instantly.

Thinking back, the phrase "making a mountain out of a molehill" comes to mind. Sure, it is upsetting to see kids being aggressive and anything but kind to each other. The real fault wasn't with my son or his behavior; it was with the way I reacted to it. This was my first big parenting lesson.

We now have our own system of discipline, firm boundaries, and rules that we expect to be followed. Of course, biting is normal in preschoolers. I now have a daughter who is currently in that same stage. The lessons that I needed to learn were really not about biting, or even about setting limits, or discipline. I had to learn to be a more intuitive parent, to consider my child as an individual, and most of all, to be his friend.

• • • • •

Meaghan McKenna-Porcelly is a writer based in the Hudson Valley region of upstate New York.

Turning the Tables

BY CRIS ROBINS

"Where have you been? Do you know what time it is? It's after one in the morning. What's the matter—you never heard of Alexander Graham Bell? You couldn't call?"

"I thought about it," came the weak reply. "But I thought you'd be asleep."

"That's no excuse. I was worried sick. Did you know I called the police? Thankfully there were no accidents tonight. I called the place you were supposed to be. They said you weren't there. Luckily, I saw you pull in. You're grounded! Those are the rules—you're late, you're grounded. No calls to friends, no going out, no movie rentals, and don't even think about playing video games. You scared me to death!"

It was the drama that goes on in so many households with teenagers. But unfortunately for me, in my household it was me who came home late and my child beset with worry.

What was I thinking? I guess that was the problem—I wasn't thinking. My nineteen-year-old son was making that painfully clear. Friday nights, the husband and I go to an auction. Usually we're home about nine. But this Friday there was a special lathe we'd been looking to buy. There was the unbearable heat. There was no excuse.

I had preached for years about the importance of calling home when you were going to be late; yet I had not heeded my own words. Just that afternoon, as I sat down for dinner, I had called the dentist's office because my son was twenty minutes late coming home. Accidents happen.

As parents we are charged with taking the very best care that we can of our children. We try to protect them from the woes of the world. We try to provide them with an environment that is secure, that is safe from harm and worry. Yet, sometimes we forget. Sometimes we show that we are ultimately only human, that we too make mistakes.

Saturday morning, as I reflected on the events of the evening, my youngest son, who's only ten, jumped out of bed and ran out to the living room to find me. He sighed with relief when he saw me drinking my morning coffee, just like every morning. It was a sign that everything was back to normal. The worry of the night was evident on his little face. It hurt me a great deal to know that I was the cause of that worry.

Saying I'm sorry, begging for forgiveness, and promises of never doing it again, all seemed so inadequate. However, it was the only course available, as I could not turn back the hands of time, and undo the deed.

As he snuggled close to me on the couch he said, "You're home safe and sound, that's all I care about." My own words, again, came back to haunt me. "But," he said, smiling up at me, "you're still grounded."

• • • • •

Cris Robins, published author and international journalist, is the sole creative force behind Writer-for-Hire (*www.writer-for-hire.com*) and several other writing-related firms. She is currently working on her M.A. in English literature from Mercy College and, while residing in St. Louis, Missouri, works conti-nentally and internationally.

Learning along the Way

By Del Sandeen

Breastfeeding is almost always the best choice for the baby. It also has numerous benefits for the mother. I know. So when I was pregnant with my first child, I decided I'd give breastfeeding a try.

My daughter was an enthusiastic nurser, so maintaining a good milk supply was no problem. But after a month or so, knowing I'd soon be heading back to work part-time, I tried pumping milk so that she could continue to get breast milk. The pumping was a disaster. I tried all the techniques in the books—relaxing, drinking water, thinking of the baby. Nothing worked. I could rarely express more than an ounce at a time. The only way for my baby to get milk was directly from my breasts.

I switched her to formula when I returned to work and soon after gave up breastfeeding entirely, and I have to admit, I felt a great sense of freedom. If my husband and I wanted a night out, all I had to do was provide enough bottles for the sitter, and my daughter could still get the benefit of warm milk.

When my second child was born, again, I breastfed. But it soon became obvious that something in my diet didn't agree with him. He would eat and then cry, sometimes for hours. Instead of taking the time to meticulously analyze my diet for the offending food (or foods), I started him on formula at two months old. He was happier and so was I. I could have made the effort to pinpoint exactly what I was eating that was upsetting him so, but how much longer would the poor child have been miserable? I just thought it best to feed him something that agreed with him . . . and me. Also, I was anxious to get back to my morning cup of coffee, which I had dutifully avoided during pregnancy. Even a few sips of caffeinated soda had caused vigorous kicking when I was pregnant, like he was angry I was having Coca-Cola, so I really felt he had no tolerance for caffeine. Once he was weaned, I was free to enjoy all the caffeinated beverages I so craved—which made it much easier to survive his regular awakening at 5:30 A.M.

And once he woke up it was mommy-and-me time. His need for constant human contact was sweet, but not always feasible. I had to cook meals, wash dishes, and fold laundry while holding him in a front carrier. Soon after he was out of his crib and sleeping in a toddler bed, he discovered that he could climb out of it and get into bed with Daddy and me. While images of mom and dad lovingly snuggled in bed with the children give lots of people warm fuzzies, I can't sleep with kids. They kick, they squirm, and sometimes snore. I need personal space, yes, even in my sleep. Plus, my son loved to sleep with his arm draped tightly around my neck. I can't rest peacefully when I feel I'm being strangled. So, I would detach the boy and carry him back to his room. I did this once a night for quite a while until he learned that he had his own bed and he had to stay in it.

Now we're on baby number three (and the final one), another sweet boy. It was quite an adjustment having him because his older brother is six years old. I've breastfed him the longest. As with his siblings before him, I need time away from my baby. Much as I love looking at his happy little face, there are times when I gladly hand him over to his big sister (who often begs to hold him anyway) and put my feet up and read.

His biggest struggle has been sleeping at night. I remember reading one child-care book that said no one was entitled to a full night's sleep. I felt like crying! I was exhausted from getting up with the baby a minimum of twice per night. I was walking around like a zombie and just wanted to feel like something more than a milk-producing machine. What I wanted more than anything in the world was to sleep more than three hours at a time. Sleep deprivation was making me irritable and grouchy.

But now he's sleeping better, and I feel more like my old self; not so foggy and forgetful. Because he is our last, I told myself to cherish every minute, but I admit, I haven't done that. It was difficult cherishing those middle-of-the-nights when we were staring at each other at three in the morning, wondering who was going to fall asleep first.

Older and wiser, I look back on some of the parenting mishaps I committed and no longer berate myself for not loving every minute. And I no longer feel guilty about needing—really needing—some time alone each day. I'm not going to regret popping in a thirty-minute Barney video for my daughter to watch while I rested on the sofa. I also commit the heinous sin of sometimes waiting for the children to go to bed before I pull out my favorite chocolates and eat them in blessed silence.

Being a mom is wonderful. There truly is no other job like it in the world—nothing as rewarding, fun, fulfilling, and yes, tiring. I know I'm not perfect, but I do the best I can. I hope my children can forgive me for letting them skip a bath now and then because I was too tired, not making them brush their teeth every single night before bed, or telling them the quarter toy machine at the grocery store was broken instead of digging for change. Hopefully, the limitless love and joy I feel for them makes up for all my shortcomings.

• • • • •

Del Sandeen lives in sunny Florida with her husband and three children. Her work has appeared in regional and national publications, as well as on the Web. She is currently writing a novel.

Thank Goodness for Chef Boyardee

By Robin Lore

I am a work-from-home mom and I mean that in the true sense of the phrase. I don't send my two toddler girls to day care and I don't employ a full-time mother's helper. When most people, men and women alike, find out that I work from home, they promptly assume that I spend most of my days baking cookies with my kids, creating great works of refrigerator art, and cooking fabulous, nutritious meals.

The truth, however, is not so wholesome. The truth is— I feed my kids SpaghettiOs, canned mini ravioli, Beefaroni, mac & cheese out of the blue box, and soup out of the red can. I do not share this information with most people, especially those who know I am an organic vegetable gardener and have been on "The Zone" diet for the last two years. But, there you go, the cat is out of the bag, or should I say the O is out of the can?

Now don't get me wrong, I'm not a big food snob and I mean no offense to those mothers who have no guilt associated with giving their kids these foods. Heck, I'm a sucker for cold

Beefaroni myself, I love the stuff. Rather, I'm a product of my old-school Italian/Irish upbringing, which practically requires that you feel guilty if you are not slaving over a hot stove for your children.

If my grandmother ever found out about my secret, she would quickly remove me from her will, or worse, fake a heart attack and not speak to me for months. My mom followed the child-rearing rules handed down to her by her mom, none of which included using a can opener to feed your kids lunch; in fact I can remember sneaking SpaghettiOs at my best friend's house after school, begging her not to tell.

But, guilt or no guilt, every day at approximately 12:30 P.M. I open the kitchen cabinet and ask my girls: "What will it be today guys, SpaghettiOs, ravioli, soup, or mac & cheese?" Why do I do this? Because it's easy. I *work* from home, really work. Contrary to popular belief this does not mean I only work when my girls are napping or on the days when my mother's helper *is* at my house. A deadline is just that and it is not going to wait for me to meet it. So, I open the can, divide it into two paper bowls and, Heaven help me, stick them in the microwave for a few minutes. My kids are happy and full, I'm less stressed, and there's no mess to clean up. Do I do this every day? No. When I'm not rushed to meet a deadline I make them whatever their little hearts desire, but on the days I'm under the proverbial gun, the Chef is my best friend.

What could be so bad about something that makes everyone involved so happy? Well, this food has just about no nutritional value whatsoever. All of it is pure carbohydrate; combine that with the lack of vegetables or fruit at lunchtime and you have a neurotic mother wondering if she is depriving her kids of good health. Although they're growing, full of energy, and have no allergies, my grandmother's voice shouts to my guilty mind at 1:00 A.M., "Oh sure they *look* fine, but are they really? How could they be if all you feed them is junk food?"

So, after struggling on my own with my opposing feelings of love and hate of all things canned for six months, I did the logical thing; I asked my pediatrician. She almost laughed out loud at my profound dismay, but, nevertheless, she asked me all the right doctor questions.

"Is that all you feed them, breakfast, lunch, and dinner?"

"Well, no, of course not," I stammered in reply.

"What do you feed them for breakfast?" she asked.

"Eggs, oatmeal, pancakes, fruit and sometimes cream of wheat." This last was mumbled quickly and under my breath as I thought of the bright red box with the bold letters screaming "Instant."

"*What*, I didn't catch that last thing you said?"

"Um, Cream of Wheat." My voice cracked like a kid who didn't study getting called on in class.

She smirked at me. "Okay, all good stuff. Now, what about snacks?"

"Yogurt, fruit, cheese and whatever's growing in the garden at any point in time, sometimes beans, tomatoes, or fresh cucumbers, carrots, and radishes." My voice was getting stronger and I was feeling bolder. "Sometimes we just go out into the garden and pick a basket full of veggies, wash them off and snack on them."

I think she winked at me then, but I'm still not sure; I could have imagined it; she did, however, smile at me. "And, what about dinner?" Now I was on a roll.

"Oh, we always eat a portion of protein, chicken, fish, tofu, beef, pork, or beans; and, of course, lots of vegetables; and a little starch like couscous, rice, or potatoes." Damn, I was practically the poster mom for good nutrition.

"Well, I don't think I have to tell you that as long as your girls are eating fruits, vegetables, and lean sources of protein most of the time, feeding them canned ravioli at lunch isn't going to hurt them. Besides, look at them, they're growing normally, full of energy, not overweight or underweight, and their teeth look great." I suppressed the urge to hug her and ask her for a note for my grandmother, but opted for a "Thanks Doc, I feel much better now."

And I really did feel better. Why I hadn't thought to ask her sooner I'll never know. Even though friends and my husband tried to tell me I was not a terrible mother because I fed my kids canned food for lunch, their voices were no match for Grandma Dorothy's.

Some time has passed since then and I've loosened up a lot since that doctor's visit. I even take the girls to Burger King every so often. I'm not nearly so hard on myself and I sleep well at night. I've even come out of the cabinet to my mom.

She wasn't nearly as upset as I imagined she would be. She just smiled, leaned forward, and whispered in my ear, "Don't tell your grandmother, sweetie."

Don't worry, Mom, I won't.

• • • • •

Robin LoRé is the mother of three daughters, all of whom are terrific, despite any blunders she imagines, and knows, she has made. She works from home as a freelance author and is currently attempting her first novel. She and her family reside in rural New Jersey.

Strength of Will

By Cate Pietro Smith

his little six-pound, twelve-ouncer is kicking my ass. My red-headed daughter, Emma Jane, born March 4, 2004, is six weeks old. I'm thirty-nine, operating on very little sleep, my emotions are jumping out from behind shadows, I have no time for myself, our household routine is nonexistent, and resentment is creeping in. I wake each morning with a mental to-do list to empty the laundry basket, clean the dishes, get the house in order, make a grocery list, grocery shop, and cook dinner. It doesn't seem like much. What was simple and easy two months ago is now an epic undertaking. My baby shows no sign of a schedule. I think this is actually harder than labor.

During labor, I had laserlike focus. I breathed so forcefully through the pain that I could have blown up hundreds of balloons. Two days earlier, I was only twenty-five percent effaced and not at all dilated. So, until my water broke at 3:19 A.M. while I labored in bed, shaking and freezing, and my contractions jumped from 5–7 minutes apart to 1–2 minutes apart, I had no idea I had come along so far so quickly. The possibility of actually not making it the hospital to deliver shocked me. I have heard stories about babies delivered on the side of the road by strangers on cell phones with 9-1-1 dispatchers, but I always attributed that to poor planning. Now, I could not imagine sitting in a moving, bouncing car for fifteen minutes, making our way from our home of three months in the charming San Diego community of Talmadge to the sterile halls of Scripps La Jolla where my husband, Andrew, was born thirty-five years ago. However, Andrew and I did make it to the hospital; as he drove our black Jetta as gently as he could at 85 miles per hour, me holding onto the ceiling handle with my right arm, using my intense breaths and the words of my hypnotherapist to remain calm during each contraction. Over and over, I repeated the mantra, "Labor is about the balance between relaxation and intensity, let go of any expectations, be open, trust your body, trust the baby." I was certain then that my baby and I could do exactly what needed to be done to get her into this world.

When my husband and I arrived at Labor and Delivery, it seemed the nurses thought I was being dramatic when I said my contractions were coming so quickly. "Honey, go into the bathroom and put on this gown. We'll examine you then and see just how far along you are." "CON-TRAC-TION!" I bellowed from behind the bathroom door each of the four times wretched pain gripped my abdomen and lower back while I changed out of my once-baggy gray sweatpants and lavender T-shirt. The contractions were coming every 30–45 seconds now. When I crept out of the bathroom with my butt peeking out from the slit in the back of the gown, the nurse suggested I get into bed. But, another contraction hit just as I lifted my leg to climb up. I stopped my ascent as the nurse prodded me to keep moving. "Can't I just stay still until the pain has passed?" I asked. She replied, "Now, honey, just get into bed, it can't be that bad, I'm sure you still have a ways to go." Three contractions and forty-five seconds later, I was in bed flat on my back. After examining me, the nurse told another nurse to call my doctor immediately and she turned to me asking, "How are you staying so calm? You're nine centimeters dilated and ready to deliver!"

I had stayed calm by sheer will, I am certain of it, and six weeks later I know I still have it inside me. But, I'm so tired now and trapped. I simmer in frustration in the late afternoon when I have not touched anything on my to-do list, and, in the middle of these past few nights, anger boils over when Emma Jane wakes to be fed. My anger disturbs me. So does the fact that I'm not even waking up to her cry even though she is in her co-sleeper right next to me. Andrew always wakes, however, and changes her then wakes me to nurse.

Three nights ago, the anger was too much. I sobbed uncontrollably while Andrew and Emma Jane sat together in the butter yellow rocker in her room adorned by the same four Beatrix Potter pictures that hung in his room when he was a baby. My stomach was in knots, and shame crawled over my skin. I could not take my baby from her father to give her what she needed. As Andrew comforted Emma Jane, I turned sharply away and ran to our bedroom. I threw myself onto the foot of the bed and pounded the mattress with my fists and forearms, releasing the pent-up aggression, guilt, expectation, and tension that beat me up nightly and stole my will. After several minutes of outburst, I just sat still for a while. Tears began to flow down my cheeks and onto my lap as the words that served me so well during labor surfaced: "Let go, find your balance, trust yourself, trust Emma Jane, you will work through this, you will work it out."

I nursed Emma Jane and slept deeply for four solid hours, awaking to her cry with a clarity that had been missing for the past several weeks. I realized that morning that I have been giving this little baby all my power, that I was acting helpless. She can't even take care of herself, but somehow, I held her responsible for my well-being. She didn't deserve this. I thought to myself, "Shit, this is just the start of it!" I decided I needed to take action immediately and use my skills as a life coach on myself before the situation got entirely out of control.

That morning, I began by thinking about how I wanted to be as a mother and I wrote down the following: "I have nerves of steel; I am strong enough to handle sleep deprivation while beautifully caring for Emma Jane; my voice, words, and tone are loving, patient, and kind; my arms are a place of comfort for my daughter; my patience is at the highest it's ever been in my life; and I give myself permission to figure out this new life of mine and to love it."

Over the next few days, I realized that my foundation became shaky after bringing Emma Jane home and I needed to somehow stabilize it. I asked myself, "What can I do on a daily basis to get grounded and centered?"

The best way I know to accomplish this, even better than meditating or doing yoga, is to make decisions in my daily life based on what's most important to me. So, for now, I am going to focus on my family and give myself time to figure out my new household routine by putting away my to-do list, at least for a while. In the past, this has always led me down the path of discovery. In this case, I am certain it will help me learn what is most essential to me and my family, what is missing and how I want to spend my days. I also need some time for myself, so after Andrew gets home from work, I will take an hour away three nights a week to go on a walk, do yoga at a local studio or just sit quietly. This will also give Andrew and Emma Jane what they need to find their way as daughter and father. These are non-negotiables and where I will begin my quest to rebuild my will, take care of myself and my baby, and find my way in motherhood.

Eleven months later, I have established a household routine that is realistic and flexible; I take time for myself regularly; and I find it simple to meet my own needs. When Emma Jane wakes in the morning and from her naps, I respond to her calmly and happily; and we have quality time together every day.

My will brought me through the first year, just as it did labor. But the biggest saboteur of my will is guilt. It is more

pervasive and sneaky than just appearing in response to something I have done: it fights me the hardest when I need to be
my strongest. I ground my feet firmly with unquestionable
belief and trust in myself, especially when things are trying.
And I've found that it also helps to tell Emma Jane that I am
more stubborn and have a stronger will than she. I am convinced that by trusting this, I will stay ahead of her, if only by
a step or two at times.

• • • • •

Cate Pietro Smith writes, mothers, and lives in San Diego,
California, with her husband and one-and-a-half-year-old
daughter. A graduate of San Diego State University, she holds
a master of arts degree in education and counseling, and works
part time as a personal coach.

Jumping to Conclusions

BY SHEILA PAXTON

Very pregnant with my third child, I was taking some time to play outside with my two-year-old son. Suddenly, my four-year-old daughter started screaming from inside the house. Instead of being alarmed, I was annoyed, for this had been her reaction over broken crayons, a squashed bug, and especially if her younger brother had moved or taken a toy from her. I yanked open the screen door and yelled, "Stop screaming! For crying out loud, Shaylah, what—"

Her face was bright red with exertion, her little palms pressed to her cheeks as she danced in front of the sink screaming. A waterfall ran down from the sink, spilling hot, sudsy water all over the floor. I rushed over and turned off the sink, baffled at my short-term memory. I had started filling the sink to soak a pan when I noticed my two-year-old son staring longingly out the back door. Leaving the sink running, with full intentions of remembering it, I headed outside with my son and must have instantly forgotten about the running water.

I turned to my distraught daughter, who must have thought the house was flooding, and offered my deepest apology. I felt horrible for jumping to conclusions and wondered how much worse I would have felt had she been hurt. I dried her tears, gave her a big hug, and then covered the floor with towels in an effort to clean up my mess.

As I threw soggy towels into my washing machine, I knew that it wasn't so much what I said to Shaylah that made me feel guilty, it was the way I felt toward her that really dug a knife into my heart. Her wild screaming twisted my nerves into a ball and sent my temper flaring. I think that's what causes most mothers to feel guilt-ridden. Maybe it's not so much what we do or say to our children, but what we think about them that makes us feel horrible and unworthy of the child's love.

• • • • •

Sheila Paxton is a twenty-eight-year-old, stay-at-home mother of three (a five-year-old, two-year-old, and three-month-old). Her husband of ten years is in the Air Force and they currently reside at Seymour Johnson AFB in North Carolina. Sheila reports that motherhood is the most challenging, yet rewarding, journey she's ever been on.

The Family That Shops Together . . .

By Peggy Duffy

When my twelve-year-old daughter was working on a self-esteem unit at school, she had to list the activities she enjoyed and did well. Right up there with swimming, reading, and softball was "shop at the mall." I felt so proud.

Shopping is an exercise in self-indulgence that I have always pursued with esteem-building speed. Much to my husband's dismay, motherhood, at first, did not slow me down. In fact, it provided further opportunities.

As a stay-at-home mom, I was no longer confined to an office lunch hour. The first few months were sheer bliss—an infant is as content to be wheeled around the mall as anywhere else. But active babies and toddlers do not take well to hours of stroller restraint and that advertised "sale-of-the-year" quickly turned into the nightmare-of-the-century. My husband smiled as my buying power was sharply curtailed, forcing me to head for the park instead.

A desperate shopaholic will resort to anything. I was amazed to discover the expansion in inventory at our local supermarket.

In addition to food, medicine, and toiletries, I could purchase books, magazines, nylons, toys, baby paraphernalia, dishes, and even small appliances. I deluded myself into believing that this was real shopping. Even my daughter seemed happier sitting upright in a shopping cart at adults'-eye-view rather than strapped knee-level into a stroller.

We were a contented duo. Then one day, the child I was wheeling through the supermarket aisles decided to be cranky, fidgety, and noisy. In an attempt to quiet her, I grabbed the first thing I could from a nearby shelf, a jar of baby food. For the next three aisles, she was quiet and busy, turning the jar over and over in her plump hands until the predictable happened. The jar landed with a loud crash at my feet.

"Who would give a baby something made of glass to play with?" I heard within seconds of impact. This observation came from a middle-aged woman at the end of the aisle and it was directed to everyone within earshot.

While her eyes bored through me, I picked up the broken glass mixed with the pureed gooey mess from the floor. I could feel her pinning the "Incompetent Mother of the Year" award on me. In my heart, I knew she was right. I also knew that if I was going to put up with the sympathetic glances and critical comments, it might as well be for a worthy cause. It was time for some real shopping.

I had been a very rigid mom when it came to schedules, serving each meal at the same time and place every day as the experts advised, believing that children thrived on routine.

. . . .

When I reread the baby books, I noticed that every chapter revolved around the child's needs. Nowhere did the books acknowledge the mother's needs. Not one chapter was devoted to shopping. So I threw away the books and wrote my own chapter.

I scheduled our shopping excursions to coincide with mealtimes, my daughter happily munching away in her stroller or cart while I commando-shopped for bargains. Buoyed by early success, I was soon back on the schedule I'd had when my daughter was an infant, and the sales had never been better.

Over the next few years, one child multiplied into three. I admit that the nourishing nibbles I originally served deteriorated over time in nutritional value, yielding to sugary snacks. It seemed like the chocolate food group was introduced earlier and earlier with each child. My youngest son was weaned from bottle to lollipop. But the shopping schedule remained intact.

My children also began to enjoy our excursions a little too much and I began to feel the effects of being outnumbered. My two girls loved pushing their little brother around in his stroller, sometimes too fast. They crawled beneath the racks of clothes to play hide-and-seek. They became catalysts for each other's wild and inappropriate actions, egging each other on, not adding up to three but to some higher multiple of boundless energy and activity.

Doing any serious shopping proved interesting. I once picked out a room-sized rug in three minutes flat, while the girls unstrapped their brother from his stroller and taught him how to do somersaults on the cushioned stack of carpets. The salesman's reluctance to wait on me was apparent, especially when I asked to see the rug at the bottom of the pile. When I said, "I'll take it," the stunned look on his face told me it was the easiest and fastest commission he'd ever earned.

Buying clothes was tougher. Even candy did not provide a long enough diversion to keep them still in the dressing rooms. You haven't lived until you've attempted to keep your children entertained in ladies' underwear. They once took off for parts unknown while I was trying on bras. It is physically impossible to emerge from a dressing room in this state, so I just prayed they were too unruly for anyone to kidnap.

That was the last straw. Fortunately the timing was right. I sent one daughter off to kindergarten and the other to preschool.

My son turned out to be the ideal shopping companion. He was content to sit in his stroller for hours quietly sucking on the supply of lollipops I fed him. These also kept his hands occupied so they weren't all over the merchandise, leaving a residue of toddler gunk in their wake. This practice did leave us both vulnerable to the opinions of others, however, he to the envy of other toddlers and I to the criticism of their mothers.

There was one particularly enticing sale where a department store was going out of business and everything was reduced. Arriving early, I stood outside with the growing crowd waiting for the doors to open. Anticipation was high as we entered and fanned out in all directions. I parked the stroller in handbags and was comparing various selections when a two-year-old girl gazed openly at my son, who was on his first lollipop of the day.

"Mommy, can I have a pop?" she asked in a voice as sugary as what my son was eating. She stood well-behaved and angelic by her mother's side.

"We don't eat candy," was the haughty reply of the mother who looked at me with disdain.

Our eyes met briefly and I could read her mind: "If this sale wasn't so good, I'd call social services right now about your mistreatment of that child."

Three hours later I ran into her again—same store, shoe department. My son was neither tired, cranky, nor hungry, on a euphoric sugar high from his morning's lollipops. The shopping marathon had been a productive one. The stroller was weighed down by the shopping bags hanging from its handles. I had just finished selecting two pairs of dress shoes and a pair of sneakers (all reduced fifty percent) when I looked over and saw the girl clinging to her mother's thigh, whining and crying. The mother looked tired, worn-out, and frazzled as she simultaneously attempted to slip on some shoes and peel the child off her leg.

Our eyes met briefly. I hoped she could read my mind. "We eat lollipops" was written there.

It was inevitable. A side effect of my methods is I have created monsters—shopping monsters, that is. Maybe because my children have always associated shopping with sweet pleasure, maybe because they've spent so much of their lives in the stores. All three have evolved into ardent shoppers—even my son. Today the mall is one of their favorite outings. Whenever I head for the door, I hear, "Where are you going?" followed by a chorus of "Can I come?"

Our shopping trips are still interesting. They range from three contented kids who all want to go to the same places and do the same things (you judge, is that a fantasy or rare reality?) to three dissonant voices saying simultaneously, "I want to go to the computer store," "I'm hungry," and "I can't believe I have to be seen in public with those two." It doesn't slow us down. With the stamina of youth, they usually outlast me. These days, I'm the one who gets restless and cranky, and needs a snack.

Some mothers head for the park or the zoo or the museums with their children. Others go biking or picnicking or bowling. We've done those too, of course, but over the years my children no longer want to be seen in certain places, like standing next to a monkey cage. Dinosaur bones are boring and they'd rather bowl with their friends.

In school, they're teaching children to create positive feelings about themselves, to find healthy outlets so they don't pursue unhealthy ones. Shopping is the one family activity that seems to have endured with a passion in our house and high on my list of healthy pursuits.

• • • • •

Peggy Duffy's short stories and essays have appeared in numerous publications, including *Newsweek,* the *Washington Post, Brevity, Octavo, Drexel Online Journal, Three Candles, So to Speak, Smokelong Quarterly, Literary Mama, Cup of Comfort for Mothers and Sons,* and elsewhere. She maintains a Web site at *www.authorsden.com/peggyduffy.*

Birthday Boy

By Nora Miller

When my son was not quite three, my husband and I were both in college in Vermont, taking many of the same classes.

Our favorite was an invertebrate biology class with a really great professor who knew how to get and keep the interest of his students. That spring he scheduled a four-day field trip to Cape Cod, Massachusetts, including a visit to the famous Wood's Hole Oceanographic Institute. Although the trip was not required for a grade in the class, we both felt we couldn't pass up the opportunity. However, joining the trip would mean leaving our son with my mother. Until then, we had rarely left him alone for an evening, much less a four-day stretch, and this particular four-day stretch included his third birthday!

My mother assured us that at three years old, Nathan would not know or care that we missed the exact day. We could celebrate when we got back and everything would be fine. With some lingering reluctance, we left for our field trip. It was fabulous and we learned a lot.

When we got back to town late Sunday afternoon, we realized that we had no birthday cake for Nathan's party. A quick
call to my mother revealed that she had not gotten or made
one either. Vermont had strict "blue laws" at that time, and all
grocery stores were closed. Our only hope lay in the corner
"mini-mart" which had opened recently. Somehow it managed
to avoid the restrictions, perhaps by selling gasoline, a necessity that trumps the need for Sunday devotion. We pulled up
outside and ran in to see what they had.

Nothing. No cakes, no cake mixes, no frozen cakes. The only
thing that came even close to something festive like a cake was
a box of frozen éclairs. We looked at each other and shrugged.
Better than coming home late *and* empty-handed. Amazingly,
they did have birthday candles, including a big blue "3."

At home, Nathan was overcome by our return. Not over-
joyed—more like relieved, and maybe even a bit chastened. I
wonder, looking back, if he thought we had left him because of
some bad behavior on his part. It's tough being a kid.

We sat at the kitchen table, Nathan in my lap, my husband
close beside us. My mother made tea and coffee and warmed
up the éclairs. Nathan pulled my hands together so I was hug-
ging him. When I reached for a sip of tea, he pulled my hand
back. My guilt rose up, and I could feel my face flush. My poor
baby had missed me and I could never quite make it all better.

Then the birthday "cake" arrived, a plate of éclairs, one of
which sported a burning "3" candle. Nathan's eyes lit up and

he followed all the proper procedures—waiting patiently while we sang, pausing to make a wish, blowing out the candle, looking around proudly while we applauded his success. But the éclairs tasted like the cheap last resort that they were, and I was afraid I had scarred my son for life.

As the years passed, and Nathan's birthdays came and went, I often recalled this one disastrous birthday, a burning symbol of my inadequate mothering abilities. I never mentioned it to him, but my husband and I occasionally speculated on the possible lasting effects. He turned out all right, though, a loving son, a good student, a kid with friends, and everything else.

Sometime later, when my son reached his mid-twenties, we came upon yet another of his birthdays. Since our tradition had always been that the birthday boy got to pick the dessert, I asked him what, if anything, he wanted *this* time. He got a kind of wistful look on his face and replied, "One of my earliest memories is of a birthday at Gramma's house. There was something special about it. I don't remember why, but I do remember that we had these wonderful éclairs. It was the best birthday I can remember."

My emotions seemed to tumble over one another. I felt joy that he had such a fond memory; chagrin that it was of the same moment over which I had spent so much guilt for so many years; disbelief that I could have gotten it so wrong all these years; relief that I could stop feeling that dull-sharp twinge whenever I thought of those little hands pulling mine tight around him.

Of course, I had to tell him the whole story then. We were both amazed at how easily the "truth" becomes so individual. We each experienced that moment with the éclairs and the "3" candle, but we stored it in different mental boxes, and felt completely different emotions when the boxes were opened.

What I learned from this is that you can never predict what your child will take away from a moment. Events that seem trivial to you may loom large for them, coloring their perceptions in future similar situations. And things that you might consider *really important* will not make sense to them, or will take on an importance you didn't imagine. I learned that you can do the best you can do, but you can never assume you know what your child is thinking. If you have doubts, ask. Talk with them about the events you think might have an affect on them. If necessary, explain what they might not or could not know about the reason something happened. And don't be too hard on yourself for being inadequate now and then—those may turn out to be your shining moments!

Of course, I bought him éclairs on that recent birthday. He proclaimed them okay, but not as wonderful as those from that long-ago Sunday afternoon. I had to agree.

• • • • •

Nora Miller has loved the written word since she learned to read. An analytical streak led to a math degree, which led to a career in information systems. For twenty-five years, she wrote as many memos, letters, and reports as programs, honing her aptitude for producing clear, concise, and readable copy on a wide range of subjects. She also writes for and edits a language quarterly called *ETC,* which focuses on how language influences behavior.

Index to the Confessions

● ●

. . . .

Swearing

She learned it from me
"Lost in Toddler Translation," page 177
I said the F-word in front of her
"Mom Drops the Bomb," page 185
In front of the in-laws
"Talking Turkey," page 189

Television

I used TV as a babysitter
"Just this Once," page 124, "My Secret Weapon," page 160
I only let them watch PBS
"Letting Them Lead," page 150
I banned TV
"Television Terminator," page 154

Time

I take time for myself
"Bedtime," page 98, "Strength of Will," page 230
We sneak out on dates
"The Sick Sense," page 121
I never have enough
"Do You Have to Go to Work Today?" page 94, "Damned If You Do," page 169, "Mom's Little Helper," page 173